Sencha Touch Mobile JavaScript Framework

Build web applications for Apple iOS and Google
Android touchscreen devices with this first HTML5
mobile framework

John E. Clark

Bryan P. Johnson

[PACKT] open source*

community experience distilled

PUBLISHING

BIRMINGHAM - MUMBAI

Sencha Touch Mobile JavaScript Framework

First published: February 2012

Production Reference: 1090212

Published by Packt Publishing Ltd.
Livery Place
35 Livery Street
Birmingham B3 2PB, UK..

ISBN 978-1-84951-510-8

www.packtpub.com

Cover Image by Parag Kadam (paragvkadam@gmail.com)

Credits

Authors
John E. Clark
Bryan P. Johnson

Reviewer
Dave Kinsella

Senior Acquisition Editor
Usha Iyer

Lead Technical Editor
Alina Lewis

Technical Editors
Apoorva Bolar
Naheed Shaikh

Copy Editor
Brandt D'Mello

Project Coordinator
Michelle Quadros

Proofreader
Aaron Nash

Indexer
Rekha Nair

Graphics
Manu Joseph

Production Coordinator
Aparna Bhagat

Cover Work
Aparna Bhagat

About the Authors

John E. Clark holds a Master's Degree in Human-Computer Interaction from Georgia Tech and an undergraduate degree in Music Engineering from Georgia State University. John and his co-author, Bryan Johnson, worked together at MindSpring, and later EarthLink, starting out in technical support and documentation, before moving into application development, and finally, management of a small development team. After leaving Earthlink in 2002, John began working independently as a consultant and programmer, before starting Twelve Foot Guru, LLC, with Bryan, in 2005.

John has been working with Sencha Touch since the first early beta releases. He has also worked with Sencha's ExtJS since the early days, when it was still known as YUI-Ext.

When he is not buried in code, John spends his time woodworking, playing guitar, and brewing his own beer.

I would like to thank my family for all of their love and support. I would also like to thank Bryan for his help, his patience, and his continued faith in our efforts.

Bryan P. Johnson is a graduate of the University of Georgia. Bryan went to work for MindSpring Enterprises in late 1995, where he met his co-author John Clark. At MindSpring, and later Earthlink, for over seven years, Bryan served in multiple positions, including Director of System Administration and Director of Internal Application Development. After leaving Earthlink, Bryan took some time off to travel before joining John in starting Twelve Foot Guru.

Bryan has worked with Sencha's products since the early days of YUI-Ext and has used Sencha Touch since its first betas.

I would like to thank my family for their support and my co-author John for his patience during the creation of this book.

About the Reviewer

Dave Kinsella has been a professional web developer since 1996. Over the years, he has worked with many different technologies on projects ranging from public websites and web applications to large intranet content management systems. He has never considered himself to be a specialist in any particular field other than the general topic of "Web Technology" and spends a lot of his spare time trying out new ideas and techniques. Many of these can be found on his blog at `webdeveloper2.com`.

Dave is currently employed by Quantiv Limited, as the Head of Interactive Design, where he designs and builds flexible web-based interfaces for complex data-processing applications, using ExtJS and Sencha Touch.

www.PacktPub.com

Support files, eBooks, discount offers and more

You might want to visit www.PacktPub.com for support files and downloads related to your book.

Did you know that Packt offers eBook versions of every book published, with PDF and ePub files available? You can upgrade to the eBook version at www.PacktPub.com and as a print book customer, you are entitled to a discount on the eBook copy. Get in touch with us at service@packtpub.com for more details.

At www.PacktPub.com, you can also read a collection of free technical articles, sign up for a range of free newsletters and receive exclusive discounts and offers on Packt books and eBooks.

http://PacktLib.PacktPub.com

Do you need instant solutions to your IT questions? PacktLib is Packt's online digital book library. Here, you can access, read and search across Packt's entire library of books.

Why Subscribe?

- Fully searchable across every book published by Packt
- Copy and paste, print and bookmark content
- On demand and accessible via web browser

Free Access for Packt account holders

If you have an account with Packt at www.PacktPub.com, you can use this to access PacktLib today and view nine entirely free books. Simply use your login credentials for immediate access.

Table of Contents

Preface

Since its initial launch, Sencha Touch has quickly become the gold standard for developing rich mobile web applications with HTML5. Sencha Touch is the first HTML5 mobile JavaScript framework that allows you to develop mobile web applications that look and feel like native applications on both iPhone and Android touchscreen devices. Sencha Touch is the world's first application framework built specifically to leverage HTML5, CSS3, and JavaScript for the highest level of power, flexibility, and optimization. It makes specific use of HTML5 to deliver components such as audio and video, as well as a localStorage proxy for saving data offline. Sencha Touch also makes extensive use of CSS3 in its components and themes, to provide an incredibly robust styling layer, giving you total control over the look of your application.

Sencha Touch enables you to design both Apple iOS and Google Android applications without the need for learning multiple arcane programming languages. Instead, you can leverage your existing knowledge of HTML and CSS to quickly create rich web applications for mobile devices in JavaScript. This book will show you how you can use Sencha Touch to efficiently produce attractive, exciting, and easy-to-use web applications that keep your visitors coming back for more.

Sencha Touch Mobile JavaScript Framework teaches you all you need to get started with Sencha Touch and build awesome mobile web applications. Beginning with an overview of Sencha Touch, this book will guide you through creating a complete simple application, followed by styling the user interface and the list of Sencha Touch components, which are explained through comprehensive examples. Next, you will learn about the essential touch and component events, which will help you create rich dynamic animations. The book follows this up with information about core data packages and how to deal with data, and wraps it up with building another simple but powerful Sencha Touch application.

In short, this book has the step-by-step approach and extensive content to turn a beginner to Sencha Touch into an ace, quickly and easily.

Exploit Sencha Touch, a cross-platform library aimed at next generation, touch-enabled devices.

What this book covers

Chapter 1, Let's Begin with Sencha Touch!: This chapter provides an overview of Sencha Touch and a walkthrough of the basics of setting up the library for development. We will also talk about programming frameworks and how they can help you develop touch-friendly applications quickly and easily.

Chapter 2, Creating a Simple Application: This chapter starts out by creating a simple application and using it to discover the basic elements of Sencha Touch. We will also explore some of the more common components, such as lists and panels, and we will show you how to find common errors and fix them when they occur.

Chapter 3, Styling the User Interface: Once we have our simple application, we will explore ways to change the look and feel of individual components, using CSS styles. Then, we will dive into using Sencha Touch themes to control the look of your entire application, using SASS and Compass.

Chapter 4, Components and Configurations: Here, we will examine the individual components for Sencha Touch in greater detail. We will also cover the use of layouts in each component, and how they are used to arrange the different pieces of your application.

Chapter 5, Events: Following our look at the individual components, we will take a look at the Sencha Touch events system, which allows these components to respond to the user's touch and communicate with each other. We will cover the use of listeners and handlers, and explore ways to monitor and observe events, so that we can see what each part of our application is doing.

Chapter 6, Getting Data In: Data is a critical part of any application. Here, we will look at the different methods for getting data into our application, using forms to gather information from the user, and ways to verify and store the data. We will also talk about the different data formats that are used by Sencha Touch and how we can manipulate that data using Sencha Touch's models and stores.

Chapter 7, Getting Data Out: Once we have data in our application, we need to be able to get it back out for display to the user. Here, we will discuss the use of panels and xTemplates to display the data. We will also take a look at using our data to create colorful charts and graphs, using Sencha Touch Charts.

Chapter 8, The Flickr Finder Application: Using the information we have learned about Sencha Touch, we will create a more complex application that grabs photos from Flickr, based on our current location. We will also use this as an opportunity to talk about best practices for structuring your application and its files.

Chapter 9, Advanced Topics: For our final chapter, we will explore ways to synchronize your data with a database server by creating your own API. Additionally, we will look at ways to synchronize data between the mobile device and a database server, compiling your application with PhoneGap and NimbleKit, as well as ways to get started as an Apple iOS or Google Android developer.

What you need for this book

To accomplish the tasks in the book, you will need a computer with the following software:

- Sencha Touch 1.1
- Sencha Touch Charts 1.0
- A programming editor such as BBEdit, Text Wrangler, UltraEdit, TextMate, Aptana, Eclipse, or others
- A local web server, such as the built-in Apple OS X web server, Microsoft's built-in IIS server, or the downloadable WAMP server and software package.

Links to these items are provided in *Chapter 1, Let's Begin with Sencha Touch!*, under the section *Setting up your development environment*. Other optional, but helpful, software will be linked in specific sections when needed.

Who this book is for

This book is ideal for anyone who wants to gain the practical knowledge involved in using the Sencha Touch mobile web application framework to make attractive web applications for mobiles. If you have some familiarity with HTML and CSS, this book is for you. This book will give designers the skills they need to implement their ideas, and provide developers with creative inspiration through practical examples. It is assumed that you know how to use touchscreens, touch events, WebKit on mobile systems, Apple iOS, and Google Android for mobiles.

Conventions

In this book, you will find a number of styles of text that distinguish between different kinds of information. Here are some examples of these styles, and an explanation of their meaning.

Code words in text are shown as follows: "let's say we have an object called `wheeled vehicle`."

A block of code is set as follows:

```
<!DOCTYPE html>
<html>
  <head>
    <meta http-equiv="Content-Type" content="text/html;
charset=utf-8">
    <title>TouchStart Application - My Sample App</title>
```

When we wish to draw your attention to a particular part of a code block, the relevant lines or items are set in bold:

```
var complexTest =  new Ext.Container({
        layout: {
            type: 'vbox',
```

Any command-line input or output is written as follows:

```
C:\Ruby192>ruby -v
ruby 1.9.2p180 (2011-02-18) [i386-mingw32]
```

New terms and **important words** are shown in bold. Words that you see on the screen, in menus or dialog boxes for example, appear in the text like this: "choose the **Forum** link at the top of the page and then find the **Sencha Touch** forums".

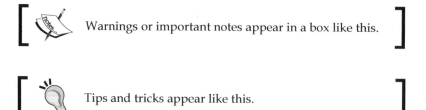

Warnings or important notes appear in a box like this.

Tips and tricks appear like this.

Reader feedback

Feedback from our readers is always welcome. Let us know what you think about this book—what you liked or may have disliked. Reader feedback is important for us to develop titles that you really get the most out of.

To send us general feedback, simply send an e-mail to feedback@packtpub.com, and mention the book title through the subject of your message.

If there is a topic that you have expertise in and you are interested in either writing or contributing to a book, see our author guide on www.packtpub.com/authors.

Customer support

Now that you are the proud owner of a Packt book, we have a number of things to help you to get the most from your purchase.

Downloading the example code

You can download the example code files for all Packt books you have purchased from your account at http://www.packtpub.com. If you purchased this book elsewhere, you can visit http://www.packtpub.com/support and register to have the files e-mailed directly to you.

Errata

Although we have taken every care to ensure the accuracy of our content, mistakes do happen. If you find a mistake in one of our books—maybe a mistake in the text or the code—we would be grateful if you would report this to us. By doing so, you can save other readers from frustration and help us improve subsequent versions of this book. If you find any errata, please report them by visiting http://www.packtpub.com/support, selecting your book, clicking on the **errata submission form** link, and entering the details of your errata. Once your errata are verified, your submission will be accepted and the errata will be uploaded to our website, or added to any list of existing errata, under the Errata section of that title.

Piracy

Piracy of copyright material on the Internet is an ongoing problem across all media. At Packt, we take the protection of our copyright and licenses very seriously. If you come across any illegal copies of our works, in any form, on the Internet, please provide us with the location address or website name immediately so that we can pursue a remedy.

Please contact us at copyright@packtpub.com with a link to the suspected pirated material.

We appreciate your help in protecting our authors, and our ability to bring you valuable content.

Questions

You can contact us at questions@packtpub.com if you are having a problem with any aspect of the book, and we will do our best to address it.

1
Let's Begin with Sencha Touch!

With the growing popularity of mobile devices, cell phones, and tablet computers, consumers have quickly moved to embrace touch-based operating systems and applications. This popularity has given developers a wide variety of platforms to choose from Apple's iOS (iPhones, iTouch, and iPad), Google's Android, Windows Mobile 7, and many more. Unfortunately, this rich variety of platforms brings with it an equally rich variety of programming languages to choose from. Picking any single language often locks you into a specific platform or device.

Sencha Touch removes this obstacle by providing a framework based in JavaScript, HTML 5, and CSS. These standards have gained strong support across most modern browsers and mobile devices. By using a framework based on these standards, you can deploy applications to multiple platforms, without having to completely rewrite your code.

This book will help familiarize you with Sencha Touch, from the basic setup to building complex applications. We will also cover some basics about frameworks and touch applications in general, as well as provide tips on how to set up your development environment and deploy your applications in a number of different ways.

In this chapter, we will cover the following:

- Frameworks
- Mobile application frameworks
- Designing applications for Touch
- Getting started with Sencha Touch
- Setting up your development environment
- Additional tools for developing with Sencha Touch

Frameworks

A **framework** is a reusable set of code that provides a collection of objects and functions that you can use to get a head start on building your application. The main goal of a framework is to keep you from reinventing the wheel each time you build an application.

A well-written framework also helps by providing some measure of consistency and gently nudging you to follow standard practices. This consistency also makes the framework easier to learn. The keys to this reusability and ease of learning are two coding concepts called **objects** and **inheritance**.

Most frameworks, such as Sencha Touch, are built around an **Object-Oriented Programming (OOP)** style. The idea behind OOP is that the code is designed around simple base objects. A base object will have certain properties and functions that it can perform.

For example, let's say we have an object called `wheeled vehicle`. Our wheeled vehicle has a few properties that are listed as follows:

- One or more wheels
- One or more seats
- A steering device

It also has a few functions:

- `Move Forward`
- `Move Backward`
- `Move Left`
- `Move Right`
- `Stop`

This is our base object. Once this base object is created, we can extend it to add more functionality and properties. This allows us to create more complex objects, such as bicycles, motorcycles, cars, trucks, buses, and more. Each of these complex objects does a lot more than our basic wheeled object, but it also inherits the properties and abilities of that original object. We can even override the original functions, such as making our `Move Forward` function go quicker for the car than for our bicycle, if needed.

This means we can build lots of different kinds of wheeled vehicles without having to recreate our original work. We can even build more complex objects. For example, once we have a generic car, we can build everything from a Volkswagen to a Ferrari, just by adding in the new properties and functions for the specific model.

Let's take a more concrete example from Sencha Touch itself—the **container** object.

The container object is one of the basic building blocks of Sencha Touch. As the name implies, it is designed to hold other items, such as buttons, fields, toolbars, and more. The container object has over 40 different configuration options that control simple things such as:

- Height
- Width
- Padding
- Margin

The configuration options also control more complex behavior, such as:

- **Layout**: Determines how items in the container will be positioned
- **Listeners**: Determine which events the container should pay attention to, and what to do when it hears the event

The container also has over 60 methods or things that it can do. These methods include simple things, such as:

- Show
- Hide
- Enable
- Disable
- Set Height
- Set Width

There are also more complex methods, such as:

- Query: Does a search for specific items within the container
- Update: Takes HTML or data, and updates the contents of the container

The container also has a number of properties that you can use and events that it can listen for.

This basic container object is used as a building block in Sencha Touch to create buttons, panels, form fields, and other more complex objects. These subobjects or child objects inherit all of the abilities and attributes of the container object (the parent object). Each will include the same configuration options for height, width, and so on. They will know how to do all the things a container can do—show, hide, and so on.

Each of these child objects will also have additional unique configurations and methods of their own. For example, buttons have an additional text property that sets their title, and buttons can also tell when a user clicks on them. By extending the container object, the person creating the button only had to write code for these extra configurations and methods.

From a coding perspective, objects and inheritance mean that we can reuse a lot of our work. It also means that, when we encounter a new language such as Sencha Touch, we can use what we learn about the basic code objects to quickly understand the more complex objects.

Building from a foundation

In addition to providing reusability, frameworks also provide you with a collection of core objects and functions, commonly used to build applications. This keeps you from starting from scratch each time you begin a new application.

These code objects typically handle most of the ways a user will input, manipulate, or view data. They also cover the common tasks that occur behind the scenes in an application, such as managing data, handling sessions, dealing with different file formats, and formatting or converting different kinds of data.

Chances are, for most frameworks, any common task you wish to perform has already been accounted for and is simply awaiting your discovery. Once you are familiar with the wide range of objects and functions provided by a framework such as Sencha Touch, you can develop your applications quickly and more efficiently:

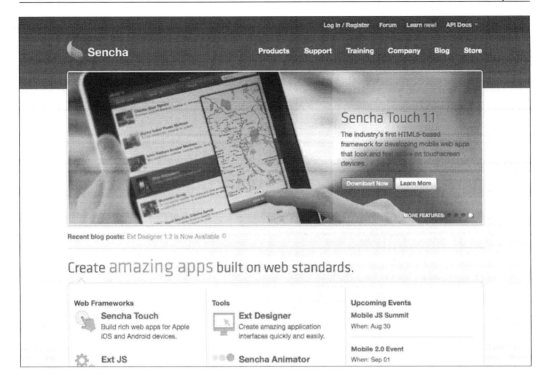

Building with a plan

One of the key things to look for in any framework is documentation. A framework with no documentation, or worse yet, one with bad documentation, is simply an exercise in frustration. Good documentation should provide low-level information about every object, property, method, and event in the framework. It should also provide more generalized information, such as examples of how the code is used in various situations.

Documentation and examples are two of the places where Sencha Touch excels as a framework. Extensive information is available on the main Sencha website, http://www.sencha.com, under **API Docs | Sencha Touch**.

A well-designed framework also maintains a set of standards and practices. These can be simple things like using camel case for variable names (for example, myVariable) or more complex practices for commenting on and documenting the code. The key to these standards and practices is consistency.

Consistency allows you to quickly learn the language and understand intuitively where to find the answers to your questions. It's a little like having a plan for a building; you understand how things are laid out and how to get where you need to go quickly.

A framework will also help you understand how to structure your own applications by providing an example for both structure and consistency in coding.

In this regard, Sencha has made every effort to encourage consistency, observe standards, and provide extensive documentation for the Sencha Touch framework. This makes Sencha Touch a very effective first language for the beginning programmer.

Building with a community

Frameworks seldom exist in isolation. Groups of developers tend to collect around specific frameworks and form communities. These communities are fantastic places to ask questions and learn about a new language.

As with all communities, there are a number of unwritten rules and customs. Always take the time to read through the forum before posting a question, just in case the question has already been asked and answered.

Sencha Touch has an active developer community with a forum that can be accessed from the main Sencha website: http://www.sencha.com/ (choose the **Forum** link at the top of the page, and then find the **Sencha Touch** forums).

Mobile application framework

Mobile application frameworks need to address different functionalities from a standard framework. Unlike a traditional desktop application, mobile devices deal with touches and swipes instead of mouse clicks. The keyboard is part of the screen, which can make traditional keyboard navigation commands difficult, if not impossible. In order to understand these constraints, we can begin by looking at different types of mobile frameworks and how they work.

Native application versus web application

There are two basic types of mobile application framework: one that builds **native applications** and one that builds **web-based applications**, such as Sencha Touch.

A native application is one that is installed directly on the device. It typically has more access to the device's hardware (camera, GPS, positioning hardware, and so on) and to other programs on the device, such as the address book and photo album. Updates to a native application typically require each user to download a new copy of the updated program.

Web-based applications, as the name implies, require a public web server that your users will access, to use the application. Users will navigate to your application website using the browser on their mobile device. As the application runs inside the web browser, it has less access to the local file system and hardware, but it also doesn't require the user to walk through a complex download and installation process. Updates to a web-based application can be accomplished by making a single update to the public web server. The program then updates automatically for anyone who accesses the site.

Web-based applications can also be modified to behave more like a native application or even be compiled by a separate program to become a full native application:

For example, users can navigate to the web application and then choose to save it to the desktop of their mobile device. This places an icon on the screen, just like a native application. It also removes the browser navigation from the application, making the application appear just like a full native application. A properly designed web application can use the device's built-in storage capabilities to store data locally and even function when the device is offline.

If you find that you need the full functionality of a native application, external compilers such as PhoneGap (http://www.phonegap.com/) can take your web-based application and compile it into a full native application that you can upload and sell in Apple's App Store or Google's Android Marketplace. PhoneGap also supplies programming hooks for you to access camera functionality, contact lists, and more.

Web-based mobile frameworks

A web-based mobile framework depends on the web browser to run the application. This is a critical piece of information for a couple of reasons.

First, the web browser has to be consistent across mobile platforms. If you have previously done any website development, you are familiar with the painful issue of browser compatibility. A website can look completely different, depending on the browser. JavaScript that works in one browser doesn't work in another. People also tend to hold on to older browsers without updating them. Fortunately, these problems are less of an issue with most mobile devices, and no problem at all for iOS and Android.

The web browser for both Apple's iOS and Google's Android is based on the **WebKit** engine. WebKit is an open source engine that basically controls how the browser displays pages, handles JavaScript, and implements web standards. What this means for you is that your application should work the same on both platforms.

However, mobile devices that do not use WebKit (such as Windows Mobile) will be unable to use your application. The good news is that, as more browsers adopt HTML5 standards, this problem may also begin to disappear.

The second consideration for a web-based application is where it lives. A native application gets installed on the user's device. A web-based application needs to be installed on a public server. Users will need to be able to type a URL into their web browser and navigate to your application. If the application only exists on your computer, then you are the only one who can use it. This is great for testing, but if you want to have other people using your application, you will need to have it hosted on a public server.

The third consideration is connectivity. If a user cannot connect to the Internet, then they won't be able to use your application. However, Sencha Touch can be configured to store your application, and all of its data, locally. At first glance, this ability seems to negate the problem of connectivity altogether, but it actually causes problems when users connect to your application with more than one device:

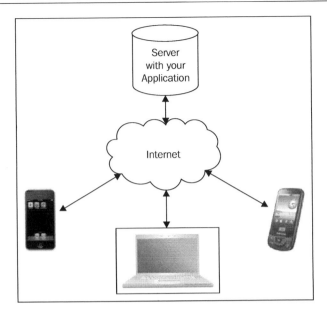

A web-based application can be accessed from anywhere, with a web browser. The same application can be accessed from a mobile device, a personal computer, and a cell phone. This is a huge advantage for information-rich applications. For example, in a web-based application, if I enter data into the application on my phone, I can log in from my home computer and still see that data. This is because the data is stored on the remote server with the application.

However, if I have set up my application to store everything locally, anything that I enter in my cell phone stays within the cell phone and cannot be viewed from another location, such as my home computer. If I use a computer to access the site, it will create a second separate local set of data, tied to my home computer.

Fortunately, Sencha Touch can be set up to synchronize data between the server and the various devices. When your application is connected to the Internet, it will synchronize any existing offline data and use the remote server for storage of anything done while online. This makes sure that your data is accessible to you across all of your devices, while allowing you to work offline as needed.

Web frameworks and touch

Standard web frameworks have previously been designed to work within a mouse and keyboard environment, but mobile web frameworks also have to understand the concept of touch for both navigation and data entry:

Most touch-based frameworks understand the following types of touch gestures:

- **Tap**: A single touch on the screen
- **Double tap**: Two quick touches on the screen
- **Swipe**: Moving a single finger across the screen from left to right or top to bottom
- **Pinch** or **spread**: Touching the screen with two fingers and bringing them together in a pinching motion, or spreading them apart to reverse the action
- **Rotate**: Placing two fingers on the screen and twisting them clockwise or counter clockwise, typically to rotate an object on screen

These touch interactions were initially limited to native application frameworks, but Sencha Touch and other web-based frameworks have made them available to the web browser.

Now that we can use these touches and gestures for our mobile applications, we should also consider how they change the way our users will interact with our applications. We should also talk a bit about the potential issues with mobile applications in general.

Designing applications for mobile and touch

Mobile applications require some changes in thinking. The biggest consideration is one of scale. If you are used to designing an application on a 21 inch monitor, dealing with a 3.5 inch phone screen can be a painful experience. Phones and mobile devices also use a variety of screen resolutions:

- **iPhone 4** and **iPod Touch 4**: 960 x 640
- **iPhone 4** and **iPod Touch 3**: 480 x 320
- **Android 4 Phones** support four general sizes:
  - xlarge screens are at least 960 x 720
  - large screens are at least 640 x 480
  - normal screens are at least 470 x 320
  - small screens are at least 426 x 320
- **iPad**: 1024 x 768

When designing a mobile application, it's usually a good idea to mock up the design to get a better idea of scale and where your various application elements will go. There are a number of good layout programs available to help you with this:

- Omni Graffle for the Mac (`http://www.omnigroup.com/products/omnigraffle/`)
- Balsamiq Mockups for Mac, Windows, and Linux (`http://balsamiq.com/`)
- DroidDraw for Mac, Windows, and Linux (`http://www.droiddraw.org/`)
- iMockups for the iPad (`http://www.endloop.ca/imockups/`)

Touch applications also have certain considerations to keep in mind. If you are coming from a typical web development background, you might be used to using events such as hover.

Hover is typically used in web applications to alert the user that an action can be performed or to provide tool tips. For example, showing that an image or text can be clicked by changing the color when the user hovers the mouse cursor. As touch applications require the user to be in contact with the screen, there really is no concept of hovering. Objects that the user can activate or interact with should be obvious and icons should be clearly labeled.

Unlike mouse-driven applications, touch applications are also typically designed to mimic real world interactions. For example, turning the page of a book within a touch application is usually accomplished by swiping your finger across the page horizontally, in much the same way you would in the real world. This encourages exploration of the application, but it also means that coders must take special care with any potentially destructive actions, such as deleting an entry.

While it may seem like programming for touch requires quite a bit of extra work and care, there are a number of advantages.

Why touch?

Before the advent of touch screens, applications were generally limited to input from external keyboards and the mouse. Neither of these is very desirable in a mobile platform. Even when full internal keyboards are used in non-touch based devices, they can take up a tremendous amount of space on the device, which in turn limits the available screen size. By contrast, a touch-based keyboard disappears when it isn't needed, leaving a larger screen area available for display.

Slide out keyboards on mobile devices do not adversely affect the screen size, but they can be cramped and uncomfortable to use. Additionally, a touch screen keyboard allows for application-specific keyboards and keys, such as the addition of the *.com* key when using a web browser.

Keyboards and mice also present a mental disconnect for some users. Using a mouse on your desk to control a tiny pointer on a separate screen often leads to a sense that you are not entirely in control over the activity. Whereas directly touching an object on the screen and moving it, places you at the center of the activity. Because we interact with the physical world by touching and moving objects by hand, a touch-based application often provides a more intuitive **User Interface (UI)**.

Touch technology is also beginning to make inroads into the desktop computer arena. As this technology becomes cheaper and more common, the need for touch-based applications will continue to grow.

Getting started with Sencha Touch

When getting started with any new programming framework, it's a good idea to understand all of the resources available to you. Buying this book is a great start, but there are additional resources that will prove invaluable to you as you explore the Sencha Touch framework.

Fortunately for us, the Sencha website provides a wealth of information to assist you at every stage of your development.

The API

The Sencha Touch **Application Programming Interface (API)** documentation provides detailed information on every single object class available to you with Sencha Touch. Every class in the API includes detailed documentation for every configuration option, property, method, and event, for that particular class. The API also includes short examples and other helpful information.

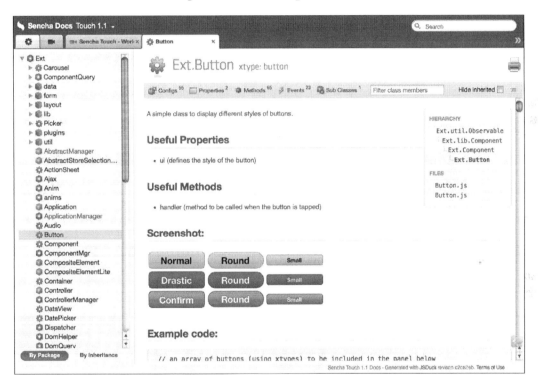

The API documentation is available on the Sencha website, `http://docs.sencha.com/touch/1-1/`.

A copy is also included as part of the Sencha Touch framework that you will download to create your applications.

Examples

The Sencha website also includes a number of example applications for you to look at. By far, the most helpful of these is the Kitchen Sink application:

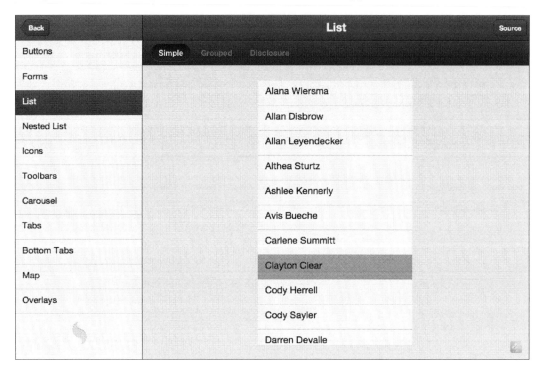

The Kitchen Sink application

The Kitchen Sink application provides examples for:

- User interface items, such as buttons, forms, toolbars, lists, and more
- Animations for things such as flipping pages or sliding in a form
- Touch events, such as, tap, swipe, and pinch
- Data handling for JSON, YQL, and AJAX
- Media handling for audio and video
- Themes to change the look of your application

Each example has a **Source** button in the upper-right corner, that will display the code for the current example.

The Kitchen Sink application also provides an **Event Recorder** and an **Event Simulator**. These will allow you to record, store, and play back any touch events fired by the device's screen.

These simulators demonstrate how to record actions inside your own application for playback as a live demonstration or a tutorial. It can also be used for easily repeatable testing of functionality.

You can play around with the Kitchen Sink application on any mobile device or on a regular computer, using Apple's Safari web browser. The Kitchen Sink application is available on the Sencha website, `http://dev.sencha.com/deploy/touch/examples/kitchensink/`.

A copy of the Kitchen Sink application is also included as part of the Sencha Touch framework that you will download to create your applications.

Learn

Sencha also has a section of the site devoted to more detailed discussions of particular aspects of the Sencha Touch framework. The section is appropriately titled **Learn**. This section contains a number of tutorials, screencasts, and guides, available for you to use. Each section is labeled as **Easy, Medium,** or **Hard,** so that you have some idea about what you are getting into.

The **Learn** section is available on the Sencha Website, at `http://www.sencha.com/learn/touch/`.

Forums

Though mentioned before, the Sencha Forums are worth mentioning again. These community discussions provide general knowledge, bug reporting, question-and-answer sessions, examples, contests, and more. The forums are a great place to find answers from people who use the framework on a daily basis.

Setting up your development environment

Now that you've familiarized yourself with the available Sencha Touch resources, the next step is to set up your development environment and install the Sencha Touch libraries.

In order to start developing applications using Sencha Touch, it is highly recommended that you have a working web server where you can host your application. It's possible to develop Sencha Touch applications, viewing local folders with your web browser. Without a web server you won't be able to test your application using any mobile devices.

Set up web sharing on Mac OSX

If you are using Mac OSX, you already have a web server installed. To enable it, launch your system preferences, choose **Sharing**, and enable **Web Sharing**. If you haven't done so already, click on **Create Personal Website Folder**, to set up a web folder in your home directory. By default, this folder is called Sites, and this is where we will be building our application:

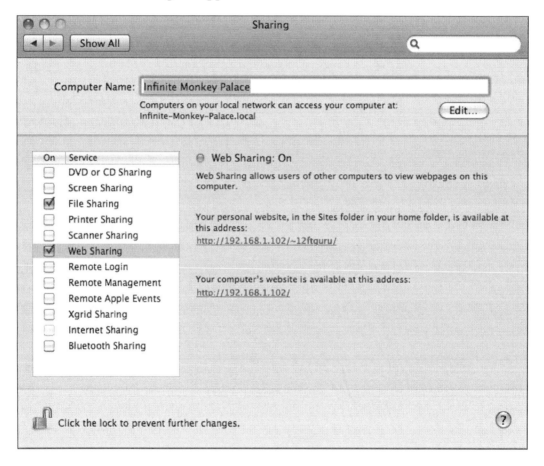

The sharing panel will tell you your web server URL. Remember this for later.

Install a web server on Microsoft Windows

If you're running Microsoft Windows, you may be running Microsoft's Internet Information Server (**IIS**). You can find out by going into your **Control Panel** and choosing either of the following options:

- **Program Features | Turn Windows features on or off** (In Vista or Windows 7). Detailed instructions are at `http://www.howtogeek.com/howto/ windows-vista/how-to-install-iis-on-windows-vista/`.

- **Add/Remove Programs | Add/Remove Windows Components** (in Windows XP). Detailed instructions are at `http://www.webwiz.co.uk/kb/ asp-tutorials/installing-iis-winXP-pro.htm`.

If you do not have IIS installed, or you are unfamiliar with its operation, we recommend installing the Apache server for use with this book. This will allow us to provide consistent instruction for both Mac and PC, in our examples.

One of the easiest ways to install Apache is to download and install the XAMPP software package (`http://www.apachefriends.org/en/xampp-windows.html`). This package includes Apache as well as PHP and MySQL. These additional programs can be helpful as your skills grow, allowing you to create more complex programs and data storage options.

After you've downloaded and run XAMPP, you'll be prompted to run the XAMPP Control Panel. You can also run the XAMPP Control Panel from the Windows **Start** menu. You should click on **Start** on the Apache line of the control panel to start your web server. If you receive a notice from your firewall software, you should choose the option to allow Apache to connect to the Internet:

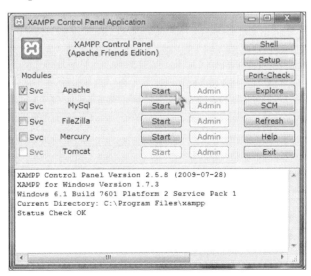

In the folder where you installed XAMPP, is a subdirectory called `htdocs`. This is the web folder where we will be setting up Sencha Touch. The full path is usually `C:\xampp\htdocs`. Your web server URL will be `http://localhost/`, and you'll want to remember this for the next step.

Download and install the Sencha Touch framework

In your web browser, go to `http://www.sencha.com/products/touch/` and click the **Download** button. Save the ZIP file to a temporary directory.

 Please note that all examples in this book were written using Sencha Touch version 1.1.0.

Unzipping the file you downloaded will create a directory called `sencha-touch-version` (in our case it was `sencha-touch-1.1.0`). Copy this directory to your web folder and rename it, dropping the version number and leaving just `sencha-touch`.

Now, open up your web browser and enter your web URL, adding `sencha-touch` to the end. You should see the following Sencha Touch demo page:

Congratulations! You've successfully installed Sencha Touch.

Additional tools for developing with Sencha Touch

In addition to configuring a web server and installing the Sencha Touch libraries, there are some additional development tools that you may want to take a look at, before diving into your first Sencha Touch application. Sencha has several other products you may find useful to use in your Sencha Touch app, and there are quite a few third party tools that can help you develop and deploy your app. We're not going to go into a lot of detail on how to set them up and use them, but these tools are definitely worth looking into.

Safari Web Inspector

Bundled with the desktop version of the Safari web browser, the Safari Web Inspector allows you to debug JavaScript and CSS, inspect HTML and your browser's local storage, and much more.

We recommend using Safari to examine your Sencha Touch application during development, and the Safari Web Inspector is a huge part of that. Both Chrome and Firefox have similar tools (Chrome Developer Tools and Firebug for Firefox), but as iOS devices use Safari for their web browser, we feel that using Safari for your development helps keep things simple and provides a consistent browsing experience. You can download it at `http://www.apple.com/safari/download/`.

We will be using the Safari web browser for testing our examples throughout this book:

In addition to Safari and the Web Inspector, there are a number of additional packages that you can use to enhance and test your own projects.

Other Sencha products

Sencha offers several products that expand the capabilities of Sencha Touch.

Sencha Animator

Although Sencha Touch comes with a few built-in animations, with the Sencha Animator desktop application, you can create professional animations that rival Flash-based animations. Unlike Flash animations, though, Sencha Animator animations run on most mobile browsers, making them perfect for adding extra flare to your Sencha Touch application. You can download Sencha Animator at `http://www.sencha.com/products/animator/`.

Sencha.io

Sencha.io is Sencha's cloud computing service offering. Their initial service is called Sencha.io Src and is a great way to incorporate images into your Sencha Touch application. Sencha.io Src handles resizing, caching, and optimizing your images across the various displays and resolutions used in mobile devices. You create a single, high-resolution image, and Sencha.io Src handles the rest. It is available at `http://www.sencha.com/products/io/`.

Sencha Touch Charts

Sencha Touch Charts brings powerful charting functionality to a touch environment, with interactive functionality aimed directly at mobile devices. Create pie charts and line, stacked, bar, and radar graphs, and easily fit them into your Sencha Touch application. Sencha Touch Charts is available at `http://www.sencha.com/products/touch/charts`:

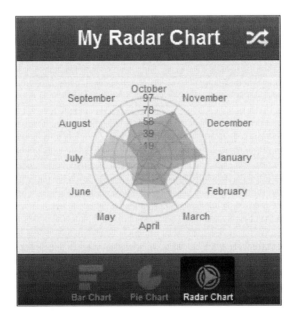

RemoteJS and EventRecorder

RemoteJS and EventRecorder are not official Sencha products, but they were developed by Sencha and released as open source tools for debugging applications running specifically on Android platforms.

RemoteJS allows you to perform remote debugging, using the Android SDK's built-in emulator or your own Android device. Then, you can execute JavaScript commands, through the RemoteJS interface, to inspect variables, and can run functions to see their output.

EventRecorder allows you to record user interactions with your application, and then play those interactions back at a later time. This allows you to test updates to your application in a repeatable, automated manner, similar to the web application testing tool Selenium.

Both RemoteJS and EventRecorder can be downloaded at `https://github.com/senchalabs/android-tools`.

Third-party developer tools

You can also choose from a variety of developer tools, which you may find useful in developing your Sencha Touch apps.

Xcode 4

Xcode 4 is Apple's complete development environment, designed for people writing for any Apple platform—OSX, iPhone, or iPad. As such, it comes with a lot of stuff that is not really necessary for writing Sencha Touch applications. However, one thing that is included with Xcode 4, that can be very handy for Sencha Touch developers, is the **iOS Simulator**. With the iOS Simulator, you can test your application on various iOS devices, without having to actually own them.

Downloading Xcode 4 requires membership in the Apple Developer program. Once you've signed up for membership, you can download Xcode 4 from `http://developer.apple.com/xcode/`:

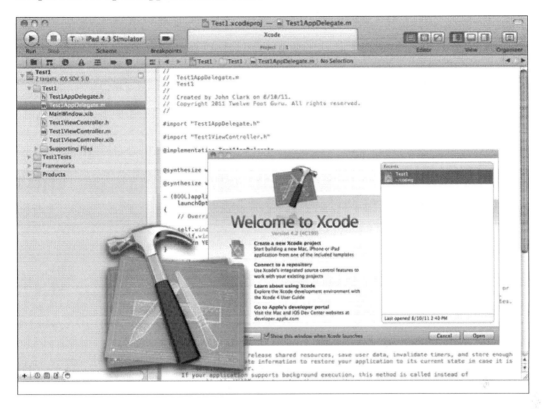

Android Emulator

Android Emulator is the Android counterpart to the iOS Simulator that comes with Xcode 4. Android Emulator is part of the free Android SDK download (`http://developer.android.com/guide/developing/devices/emulator.html`). Android Emulator can be configured to mimic many specific Android mobile devices, allowing you to test your application across a broad range of devices:

YUI test

A common part of any kind of programming is testing. **YUI test**, a part of Yahoo's YUI JavaScript library, allows you to create and automate unit tests, just as JUnit for Java does. Unit tests set up test cases for specific segments of code. Then, if in the future, that code changes, the unit tests can be re-run to determine if the code still passes. This is very useful, not only for finding errors in code, but also for ensuring code quality before a release. YUI test can be found at `http://yuilibrary.com/yui/docs/test/`.

Jasmine

Jasmine is a testing framework similar to YUI test, but based on **Behavioral Driven Design (BDD)**. In BDD testing, you start with specifications, stories about what your application should do in certain scenarios, and then write code that fits those specifications. Both YUI test and Jasmine accomplish the same goals of testing your code, just in different ways. Download Jasmine at `http://pivotal.github.com/jasmine/`.

JSLint

Possibly the most useful JavaScript tool on this list, **JSLint** will examine your code for syntax errors and code quality. Written by Douglas Crockford, one of the fathers of JavaScript, JSLint will examine your code in great detail, which is great for finding errors before you deploy your code. Download it at `http://www.jslint.com/lint.html`.

Weinre

One of the biggest problems with testing web applications on mobile devices is the lack of debugging tools. Emulators and simulators will get you most of the way there, but there are always problems that you will only encounter when you actually test on mobile devices. **Weinre** is an open source product from PhoneGap that provides you a debug console similar to the Safari Web Inspector, but for web applications running on mobile devices. It involves setting up a special server, but the instructions on the site are pretty straightforward, and the benefits very much outweigh the effort it takes to install. Weinre is available at `http://phonegap.github.com/weinre/`.

Summary

In this chapter, we've covered the fundamentals of web application frameworks and why you should use Sencha Touch. We walked through setting up a development environment and installing the Sencha Touch libraries. We also took a brief look at some of the considerations in developing touch applications and some tools to make your development life easier. You can find information at:

- Sencha Touch Learning Center (`http://www.sencha.com/learn/touch/`)
- Apple's iOS Human Interface Guidelines (`http://developer.apple.com/library/ios/#documentation/UserExperience/Conceptual/MobileHIG/Introduction/Introduction.html`)—an in depth guide to developing user interfaces for iOS devices.

In the next chapter, we'll create our first Sencha Touch application and, in the process, learn the basics of using Sencha Touch.

2

Creating a Simple Application

This chapter will walk you through creating a simple application in Sencha Touch. We will cover the basic elements that are included in any Sencha Touch application, and we will take a look at the more common components you might use in your own applications: containers, panels, lists, toolbars, and buttons.

In this chapter, we will cover:

- Setting up your folder structure
- Starting from scratch with TouchStart.js
- Controlling the container using layouts
- Testing and debugging the application
- Updating the application for production
- Putting the application into production

Next, we will cover how to use the various containers to display text and other items. We will then add additional components to create our first simple application. Finally, we will take a look at debugging your application and give you some pointers on what to do when things go boom.

Setting up your folder structure

Before we get started, you need to be sure that you've set up your development environment properly, as outlined in the previous chapter.

Root folder

As noted in the previous chapter, you will need to have the folders and files for your application located in the correct web server folder, on your local machine.

On the Mac, this will be the Sites folder in your Home folder.

On Windows, this will be C:\xamp\htdocs (assuming you installed **xampp**, as described in the previous chapter).

Through the rest of the book, we will refer to this folder as the **root folder** of your local web server.

Setting up your application folder

Before we can start writing code, we have to perform some initial set up, copying in a few necessary resources and creating the basic structure of our application folder. This section will walk you through the basic setup for the Sencha Touch files, creating your style sheets folder, and creating the index.html file.

1. Locate the Sencha Touch folder you downloaded in the previous chapter.

   The code in this chapter was written using Sencha Touch 1.1.0.

2. Create a folder in the root folder of your local web server. You may name it whatever you like. I have used the folder name TouchStart in this chapter.

3. Create three empty sub folders called lib, app, and css in your TouchStart folder.

4. Now, copy the resources and src folders, from the Sencha Touch folder you downloaded earlier, into the TouchStart/lib folder.

5. Copy the following files from your Sencha Touch folder to your TouchStart/lib folder:

   ○ sencha-touch.js

   ○ sencha-touch-debug.js

   ○ sencha-touch-debug-w-comments.js

6. Create an empty file in the `TouchStart/css` folder called `TouchStart.css`. This is where we will put custom styles for our application.

7. Create an empty `index.html` file in the main `TouchStart` folder. We will flesh this out in the next section.

Icon files

Both iOS and Android applications use image icon files for display. This creates pretty rounded launch buttons, found on most touch-style applications.

If you are planning on sharing your application, you should also create PNG image files for the launch image and application icon. Generally, there are two launch images, one with a resolution of 320 x 460 px, for iPhones, and one at 768 x 1004 px, for iPads. The application icon should be 72 x 72 px. See Apple's *iOS Human Interface Guidelines* for specifics, at `http://developer.apple.com/library/ios/#documentation/userexperience/conceptual/mobilehig/IconsImages/IconsImages.html`.

When you're done, your folder structure should look as follows:

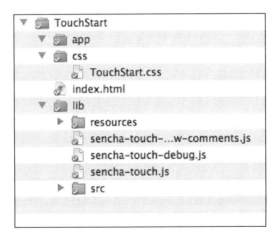

Creating the HTML application file

Using your favorite HTML editor, open the `index.html` file we created when we were setting up our application folder. This HTML file is where you specify links to the other files we will need in order to run our application.

The following code sample shows how the HTML should look:

```html
<!DOCTYPE html>
<html>
  <head>
    <meta http-equiv="Content-Type" content="text/html;
charset=utf-8">
    <title>TouchStart Application - My Sample App</title>

    <!-- Sencha Touch CSS -->
    <link rel="stylesheet" href="lib/resources/css/sencha-touch.css"
type="text/css">

    <!-- Sencha Touch JS -->
    <script type="text/javascript" src="lib/sencha-touch-debug.js"></
script>

    <!-- Application JS -->
    <script type="text/javascript" src="app/TouchStart.js"></script>

    <!-- Custom CSS -->
    <link rel="stylesheet" href="css/TouchStart.css" type="text/css">

  </head>
  <body></body>
</html>
```

Downloading the example code

You can download the example code files for all Packt books you have purchased from your account at http://www.PacktPub.com. If you purchased this book elsewhere, you can visit http://www.PacktPub.com/support and register to have the files e-mailed directly to you.

Comments

In HTML, anything between <!-- and --> is a comment, and it will not be displayed in the browser. These comments are to tell you what is going on in the file. It's a very good idea to add comments into your own files, in case you need to come back later and make changes.

Let's take a look at this HTML code piece-by-piece, to see what is going on in this file.

The first five lines are just the basic set-up lines for a typical web page:

```
<!DOCTYPE html>
<html>
  <head>
    <meta http-equiv="Content-Type" content="text/html;
charset=utf-8">
    <title>TouchStart Application - Hello World</title>
```

With the exception of the last line containing the title, you should not need to change this code for any of your applications. The title line should contain the title of your application. In this case, `TouchStart Application - Hello World` is our title.

The next few lines are where we begin loading the files to create our application, starting with the Sencha Touch files.

The first file is the default CSS file for the Sencha Touch library—`sencha-touch.css`.

```
    <link rel="stylesheet" href="lib/resources/css/ext-touch.css"
type="text/css">
```

> **CSS files**
>
> **CSS** or **Cascading Style Sheet** files contain style information for the page, such as which items are bold or italic, which font sizes to use, and where items are positioned in the display.

The Sencha Touch style library is very large and complex. It controls the default display of every single component in Sencha Touch. It should not be edited directly.

The next file is the actual Sencha Touch JavaScript library. During development and testing, we use the debug version of the Sencha Touch library, `sencha-touch-debug.js`:

```
    <script type="text/javascript" src="lib/sencha-touch-debug.js"></
script>
```

The debug version of the library is not compressed and contains comments and documentation. This can be helpful if an error occurs, as it allows you to see exactly where in the library the error occurred.

When you have completed your development and testing, you should edit this line to use `sencha-touch.js` instead. This alternate file is the version of the library that is optimized for production environments and takes less bandwidth and memory to use; but, it has no comments and is very hard to read.

Neither the `sencha-touch-debug.js` nor the `sencha-touch.js` files should ever be edited directly.

The next two lines are where we begin to include our own application files. The names of these files are totally arbitrary, as long as they match the name of the files you create later, in the next section of this chapter. It's usually a good idea to name the file the same as your application name, but that is entirely up to you. In this case, our files are named `TouchStart.js` and `TouchStart.css`.

```
<script type="text/javascript" src="app/TouchStart.js"></script>
```

This first file, `TouchStart.js`, is the file that will contain our JavaScript application code.

The last file we need to include is our own custom CSS file, called `TouchStart.css`. This file will contain any style information we need for our application. It can also be used to override some of the existing Sencha Touch CSS styles.

```
<link rel="stylesheet" href="resources/css/TouchStart.css"
type="text/css">
```

This closes out the `</head>` area of the `index.html` file. The rest of the `index.html` file contains the `<body></body>` tags and the closing `</html>` tag.

If you have any experience with traditional web pages, it may seem a bit odd to have empty `<body></body>` tags, in this fashion. In a traditional web page, this is where all the information for display would normally go.

For our Sencha Touch application, the JavaScript we create will populate this area automatically. No further content is needed in the `index.html` file, and all of our code will live in our `TouchStart.js` file.

So, without further delay, let's write some code!

Starting from scratch with TouchStart.js

Let's start by opening the `TouchStart.js` file and adding the following:

```
new Ext.Application({
name: 'TouchStart',
launch: function() {
```

```
var hello = new Ext.Container({
fullscreen: true,
html: '<div id="hello">Hello World</div>'
    });

this.viewport = hello;
    }
});
```

This is probably the most basic application you can possibly create: the ubiquitous "Hello World" application. Once you have saved the code, use the Safari web browser to navigate to the `TouchStart` folder in the root folder of your local web server. The address should look like the following:

- `http://localhost/TouchStart/`, on the PC
- `http://127.0.0.1/~username/TouchStart`, on the Mac (username should be replaced with the username for your Mac)

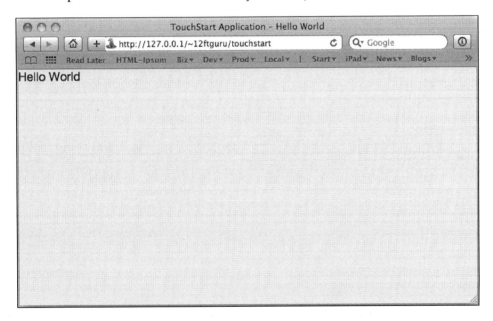

As you can see, all that this bit of code does is create a single window with the words **Hello World**. However, there are a few important elements to note in this example.

The first line, `NewExt.Application({`, creates a new application for Sencha Touch. Everything listed between the curly braces is a configuration option of this new application. While there are a number of configuration options for an application, most consist of at least the application's name and a `launch` function.

Namespace

One of the biggest problems with using someone else's code is the issue of naming. For example, if the framework you are using has an object called "Application", and you create your own object called "Application", the two functions will conflict. JavaScript uses the concept of namespaces to keep these conflicts from happening.

In this case, Sencha Touch uses the namespace `Ext`. You will see this namespace used throughout the code in this book. It is simply a way to eliminate potential conflicts between the frameworks' objects and code, and your own objects and code.

Sencha will automatically set up a namespace for your own code as part of the new `Ext.Application` object.

`Ext` is also part of the name of Sencha's web application framework called `ExtJS`. Sencha Touch uses the same namespace convention to allow developers familiar with one library to easily understand the other.

When we create a new application, we need to pass it some configuration options. This will tell the application how to look and what to do. These configuration options are contained within the curly braces ({ }) and separated by commas. The first option is as follows:

```
name: 'TouchStart'
```

This sets the name of our application to whatever is between the quotes. This `name` value should not contain spaces, as Sencha also uses this value to create a namespace for your own code objects. In this case, we have called the application `TouchStart`. The next option is where things start to get interesting:

```
launch: function() {
var hello = new Ext.Container({
fullscreen: true,
html: '<div id="hello">Hello World</div>'
    });

this.viewport = hello;
    }
```

The `launch` configuration option is actually a function that will tell the application what to do once it starts up. Let's start backwards on this last bit of code for the launch configuration and explain `this.viewport`.

By default, a new application has a viewport. The viewport is a pseudo-container for your application. It's where you will add everything else for your application. Typically, this viewport will be set to a particular kind of container object.

At the beginning of the `launch` function, we start out by creating a basic container, which we call `hello`:

```
var hello = new Ext.Container({
fullscreen: true,
html: '<div id="hello">Hello World</div>'
    });
```

Like the `Application` class, a new `Ext.Container` class is passed a configuration object consisting of a set of configuration options, contained within the curly braces ({}) and separated by commas. The `Container` object has over 40 different configuration options, but for this simple example, we only use two:

- `fullscreen` sets the size of the container to fill the entire screen (no matter which device is being used).

- `html` sets the content of the container itself. As the name implies, this can be a string containing either HTML or plain text.

Admittedly, this is a very basic application, without much in the way of style. Let's add something extra using the container's layout configuration option.

My application didn't work!

When you are writing code, it is an absolute certainty that you will, at some point, encounter errors. Even a simple error can cause your application to behave in a number of interesting and aggravating ways. When this happens, it is important to keep in mind the following:

- Don't Panic.
- Retrace your steps and use the tools mentioned in the previous chapter to track down the error and fix it. If anything from this chapter does not work for you, jump to the *Testing and debugging* section of this chapter for some pointers on where to start looking.

Controlling the container with layout

Layouts give you a number of options for arranging content inside containers. Sencha Touch offers four basic layouts for containers:

- `fit`: A single item layout that automatically expands to take up the whole container
- `hbox`: Arranges items horizontally in the container
- `vbox`: Arranges items vertically in the container
- `card`: Arranges items like a stack of cards where only the active card is initially visible

In our previous example, we did not declare a layout. In general, you will always want to declare a layout for any container. If you don't, the components inside the container may not size themselves appropriately when they appear. This is not as critical when the container only contains HTML.

Let's take our previous example and modify it a bit:

```
new Ext.Application({
name: 'TouchStart',
launch: function() {
var hello = new Ext.Container({
fullscreen: true,
layout: {
type: 'vbox',
align: 'stretch'
        },
items: [
  {
xtype: 'container',
flex: 2,
html: '<div id="hello">Hello World Top</div>',
cls: 'blueBox',
border: 1
  }, {
xtype: 'container',
flex: 1,
html: '<div id="hello">Hello World Bottom</div>',
cls: 'redBox',
border: 1
}, {
xtype: 'container',
height: 50,
```

```
html: '<div id="footer">Footer</div>',
cls: 'greenBox'
      }


      ]
    });

this.viewport = hello;
    }
});
```

For this example, we have removed the line that previously set HTML, '<div id="hello"> Hello World</div>', and replaced it with our layout configuration:

```
layout: {
type: 'vbox',
align: 'stretch'
        }
```

This configuration sets our main container layout to vbox (objects aligned vertically) and stretches the boxes to take up the full horizontal width on the screen.

We have also added items to our container, after we set the layout. The items are a collection of Sencha Touch components we want to include inside our container. The items list is enclosed in brackets, and the individual components within the items list are contained in curly braces.

In this case, we are going to include three additional containers inside of our main container:

```
items: [
  {
xtype: 'container',
flex: 2,
html: '<div id="hello">Hello World Top</div>',
cls: 'blueBox',
border: 1
  }, {
xtype: 'container',
flex: 1,
html: '<div id="hello">Hello World Bottom</div>',
cls: 'redBox',
border: 1
  }, {
xtype: 'container',
```

```
height: 50,
html: '<div id="footer">Footer</div>',
cls: 'greenBox'
  }


]
```

One of the first things you will notice is the addition of a configuration called an xtype.

In Sencha Touch, xtype: 'container' is just another way of saying new Ext. Container. This is a much easier way to add items within an existing container and has the added benefit of saving device memory. Almost every component used in Sencha Touch has a unique xtype.

xtypes

When you use xtype, the component isn't created until it is actually needed for display to the user. By contrast, any time you use the new command, such as new Ext.Container, the component is created in memory immediately.

The Sencha Touch API contains a list of the available xtype components at http://dev.sencha.com/deploy/touch/docs/ (search for *Component*).

The next configuration in the list is called flex. The flex configuration is unique to the hbox and vbox layouts. It controls how much space the component will take up, proportionally, in the overall layout. You may also have noticed that the last container does not have a flex configuration. Instead, it has height: 80. The vbox layout will interpret these values to lay out the container as follows:

1. Since we have one component with a height of 50, the vbox layout will leave that component as 50 pixels tall.

2. The vbox layout will then use the flex values of the other two components as a ratio. In this case, 2:1.

3. The end result is a container, 80 pixels high, on the bottom of the screen. The other two containers will take up the rest of the available space. The top container will also be twice as tall as the middle container.

In order to make these sizes clearer, we have also added a cls configuration to each of the inner containers. The cls configuration sets a CSS class on the container, allowing us to use our TouchStart.css file to add style changes for each of the containers.

Locate your `TouchStart.css` file, open it in your code editor, and add the following:

```
.blueBox {
background-color: #7FADCF;
}

.redBox {
background-color: #CE7E83;
}

.greenBox {
background-color: #7ECEA0;
}
```

Save your changes and reload the page in Safari:

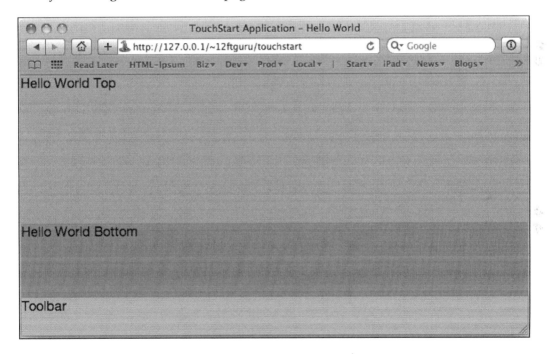

As you can see from this example, we can easily nest containers to create more complex layouts. We should also take into account the fact that each of these containers can have a different layout and can contain its own items. It would be easy enough to add buttons to our footer container on the bottom and make it into a real working toolbar. However, we really don't need to, because Sencha Touch has already provided us with a simpler way.

An important concept to understand when working with layouts is that the layout configuration does not change where the container itself lives, or how it looks, but only affects the items inside the container. Additionally, all display components in Sencha Touch have a default layout of fit. If you don't specify a different layout type, a fit layout will be used. We will cover layouts in depth, later in the book.

The panel

As we noted previously, containers are a very basic object in Sencha Touch, and they can be extended to create more complex objects with new features. The first of these is Panel.

Like the container, a panel can have a layout, html, or items components and it can be set to fullscreen. In fact, since it inherits from the container, it can do everything a container can, and more.

One of the key advantages of a panel is the ability to have docked items. These docked items can be used to make title bars, toolbars, and navigation bars. A simple example would be the following:

```
new Ext.Application({
name: 'TouchStart',
launch: function() {

  this.viewport = new Ext.Panel({
fullscreen: true,
  bodyPadding: 5,
dockedItems: [
  {
dock : 'top',
xtype: 'toolbar',
title: 'Touch Start'
  },
  {
dock : 'top',
xtype: 'toolbar',
items: [
    {
text: 'Hello Button'
    }
    ]
```

```
    }
    ],

  html: 'Hello Panel'

    });
  }
});
```

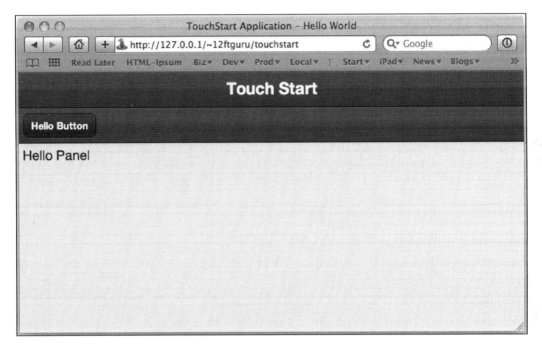

This is similar to our first example, except we are now using a panel and we have also taken a shortcut by directly setting the `viewport` method:

```
this.viewport = new Ext.Panel({
```

We also added a bit of visual appeal, in the form of padding, to the panel, by setting `bodyPadding` to 5, but the big change is the docked items.

Much like when we added containers into our main container, the docked items are shown as an array of components inside brackets. In this case, there are two items: one for the title bar and a second for the button bar. Both of these items have an `xtype` value `toolbar`.

The `toolbar` also inherits from our old friend, the container. This means it can also have `layout`, `html`, and `items` components. As a `dockedItems` component, `toolbar` also understands the concept of where it should be docked. The `dock` configuration can be set to `top`, `right`, `left`, or `bottom`.

Our first toolbar simply sets a `title` configuration value instead of `html` or `items`. However, the second toolbar is a bit different.

One of the interesting things you might have noticed in the second toolbar is that our **Hello Button** doesn't actually have a configuration value for `xtype`. This is because the toolbar assumes that all of its items are buttons, unless you tell it otherwise. In this case, the button only has a `text` property. At this point, the button doesn't do anything, but you can begin to see some of the possibilities for `panel` and its `dockedItems` component.

It should also be noted that `dockedItems` components don't have to be toolbars. They can actually be any kind of component you like. For example, if you want to have a left sidebar, you could add a `dockedItem` component with an `xtype` value of `Panel` and a `dock` setting of `left`, which would give you all the functionality of a regular panel, pinned to the left side of your existing panel.

When do I use a panel instead of a container?

Since the panel does so much more than a container, the logical question would be: why use the container at all?

The general rule of thumb is, if you need the extra functionality, use the `panel`, component, and if you don't require docked items or a title bar, use the `container` component. Using the `container` saves a bit of memory and makes for cleaner, more understandable code.

While the panel is a good starting point for starting an application, Sencha Touch also provides a more complex version of the panel called the `TabPanel`.

The TabPanel component

`TabPanel` components contain all of the core functions of the regular panel, but they have a few extra advantages as well.

`TabPanel` is a very specialized panel that uses a `card` layout to quickly create a switchable set of tabs for each item in the tab panel.

The card layout can contain a number of different containers, but it only displays them one at a time. Much like a deck of cards where only the top card is visible, the card layout can only have one active item at a time. You can then change the active item and the new card will automatically switch to the front, hiding the previous card.

The TabPanel creates a card layout for all of its items by default. It also adds a button in the tab bar for each of its items. These buttons automatically switch from one card to the next, without any additional code.

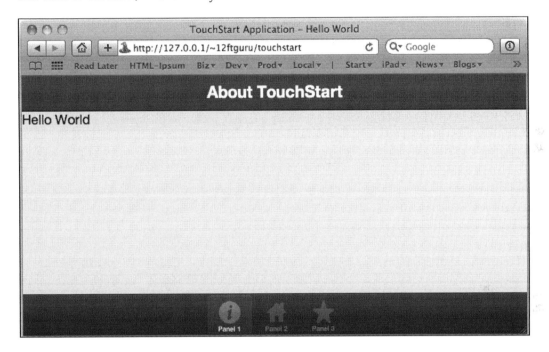

To create this new TabPanel, let's modify our previous example. Instead of setting the viewport method to a simple panel, we will set it to be a TabPanel and put our old panel inside TabPanel. We will also add two empty containers, so we can see how the tabs work:

```
new Ext.Application({
name: 'TouchStart',
launch: function() {

this.viewport = new Ext.TabPanel({
fullscreen: true,
cardSwitchAnimation: 'slide',
tabBar:{
```

```
          dock: 'bottom',
          layout: {
          pack: 'center'
                    }
                },
          items: [{
          xtype: 'panel',
          title: 'Panel 1',
          fullscreen: false,
          html: '<div id="hello">Hello World</div>',
          iconCls: 'info',
          dockedItems: [
              {
          dock: 'top',
          xtype: 'toolbar',
          title: 'About TouchStart'
              }
          ]
          }, {
          xtype: 'container',
          html: 'TouchStart container 2',
          iconCls: 'home',
          title: 'Panel 2'
          }, {
          xtype: 'container',
          html: 'TouchStart container 3',
          iconCls: 'favorites',
          title: 'Panel 3'
          }]
          });

          }
        });
```

Looking at the code, you can see that `TabPanel` has a couple of new configuration options. The first is the `cardSwitchAnimation` option, which we have set to `slide`. Other options include:

- `fade`
- `flip`
- `cube`
- `pop`
- `wipe`

You can also set this to `false`, which simply swaps the cards without any animation.

`TabPanel` also has a `tabBar` property that functions in much the same way as the `toolbar` component from our previous examples. In this example, we have set `tabBar` to appear at the bottom, and we have set the tabBar's layout to place all of the buttons together (`pack`) in the middle (`center`) of the `tabBar`.

For the `TabPanel items` list, we have our original Hello World `panel` component and a pair of simple `container` components. One difference you will see with these items is that we now have configuration options for `title` and `iconCls`. These two options control what appears on the tab for the item. `iconCls` can be set to one of the included icons, or you can customize and include your own icons.

Icons

A full list of the available icons can be found in the **Kitchen Sink** application (`http://dev.sencha.com/deploy/touch/ examples/kitchensink/`) under **Interface | Icons**. Click on the **Source** button to see how the icons are used.

Now that we have our `TabPanel` component, load the application in Safari and click through the tabs to see how they work. Change the `cardSwitchAnimation` option and see what the other options look like. You can also try changing some of the values for `iconCls`. When you are ready to move on, we will add something a bit more interesting and complex to our `TabPanel`.

The list component

The `list` component in Sencha Touch allows you to display data in a list layout. This seems pretty straightforward, but the list follows a slightly different pattern than the previous components. Let's make some modifications to our current code and see what some of those differences look like.

Find the set of parentheses that contain the first of our empty containers:

```
{
xtype: 'container',
html: 'TouchStart container 2',
iconCls: 'home',
title: 'Panel 2'
}
```

Replace that entire `container` component (including the { } at either end) with the following:

```
{
xtype: 'list',
title: 'List',
fullscreen: false,
iconCls: 'bookmarks',
itemTpl: '{id} - {fullname}',
store: new Ext.data.Store({
model: 'ListItem',
data: [
    {id: 1, fullname: 'Aaron Karp'},
    {id: 2, fullname: 'Baron Chandler'},
    {id: 3, fullname: 'Bryan Johnson'},
    {id: 4, fullname: 'David Evans'},
    {id: 5, fullname: 'John Clark'},
    {id: 6, fullname: 'Norbert Taylor'}

]
})
}
```

The first big difference we can see is that the `list` component does not declare a layout. Instead, it uses an `itemTpl` object to control how the items within the list are arranged. Notice that the elements in curly braces, `'{id} - {fullname}',`, also appear in our `data` component, at the bottom of the `list` component. This means that each row of the list will appear with the ID, a dash, and the value.

These `itemTpl` layout values are called **XTemplates** in Sencha Touch. The XTemplates consists of a string with items in curly braces. When the list appears, it will print out the XTemplates and substitute the items inside the { } with the corresponding value listed in the data.

`store` is used to control the data for the list. It can keep the data locally, as in our example, or it can retrieve the data from a server. The data within the store has to conform to a **model**. The model describes what values are available to the store and any special attributes they may have.

We will cover XTemplates, stores, and models in greater detail, later on in this book. For now, we still need to create the actual model this store example needs. Right now, the `model` configuration option for the `store` component is set to `ListItem`.

At the top of the application, create a new line right after the `launch` function:

```
launch: function() {
```

Add the following code:

```
Ext.regModel('ListItem', {
fields: [
    {name: 'id', type: 'int'},
    {name: 'fullname', type: 'string'}
  ]
});
```

This will create the correct model for our store. The model creates an array of fields, each of which has a name and a type. The name should match the one you use in the `itemTpl` object and the `data` object for the store. The `type` configuration option lets the store understand how to deal with the data when it is sorted or stored.

If everything has gone as planned, your second tab should now look as follows:

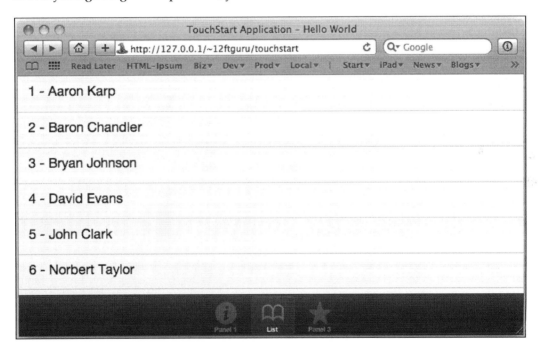

With each step of this example, we have gotten more and more complex. At some point, it is very likely that an empty screen has greeted you instead of your application. Before we go too far ahead, we need to take a look at what you should do when things go boom.

Testing and debugging the application

The first place to start when testing an application in Safari is the Error Console. From the **Develop** menu, select **Show Error Console**.

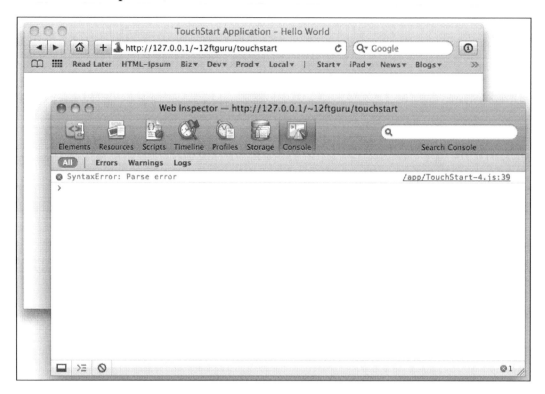

Parse errors

The Error Console in the previous screenshot tells us two very important things. The first, is that we have **SyntaxError: Parse error**. This means that somewhere in the code we did something that the browser didn't understand. Typically, this is something such as:

- Forgetting to close a parenthesis, bracket, or brace, or adding an extra one
- Not having a comma between the configuration options, or adding an extra comma
- Leaving out the semicolon at the end of one of the variable declarations
- Not closing quotes or double-quotes (also not escaping quotes where necessary)

The second critical bit of information is **/app/TouchStart-4.js: 39**. It tells us that:

- **/app/TouchStart-4.js** is the file where the error occurred
- **39** is the line where the error occurred

Using this information, we should be able to track down the error quickly and fix it.

Case sensitivity

JavaScript is a case-sensitive language. This means that if you type `xtype: 'Panel'`, you will get the following in the Error Console:

Attempting to create a component with an xtype that has not been registered: Panel

This is because Sencha Touch is expecting `panel` and not `Panel`.

Missing files

Another common problem is missing files. If you don't point your `index.html` file at your `sencha-touch-debug.js` file correctly, you will get two separate errors:

1. **Failed to load resource: the server responded with a status of 404 (Not Found)**
2. **ReferenceError: Can't find variable: Ext**

The first error is the critical bit of information; the browser could not find one of the files you tried to include. The second error is caused by the missing file and simply complains that the `Ext` variable cannot be found. In this case, it's because the missing file is `sencha-touch-debug.js`, which sets up the `Ext` variable in the first place.

Web Inspector console

Another feature of Safari Web Inspector that is incredibly useful for debugging applications is the console. In your JavaScript code, add the following command:

```
console.log('Creating Application');
```

Add it just before this new Application line:

```
new Ext.Application({
```

You should see the text **Creating Application** in your Web Inspector's console tab. You can also send variables to the console where you can view their contents, thus:

```
console.log('My viewport: %o', this.viewport);
```

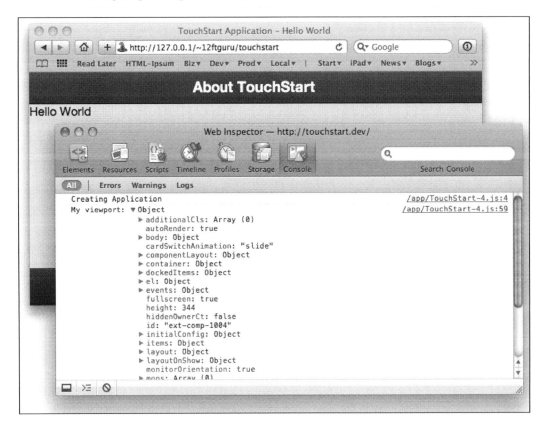

This shows you the `TabPanel` component we created, if you place it after the `this.viewport = new TabPanel` block of code. This is useful if, for some reason, you have a component that is not displaying properly. Sending an object to the console allows you to see the object as JavaScript sees it.

If you'd like to learn more about using the Safari Web Inspector for debugging your application, visit Apple's *Debugging your Website* page at `http://developer.apple.com/library/safari/#documentation/AppleApplications/Conceptual/Safari_Developer_Guide/DebuggingYourWebsite/DebuggingYourWebsite.html`.

Updating the application for production

When you're done writing and testing your application, and are comfortable that it's ready for production, there are a few simple steps you should take before you release your application into the wild.

Point to production library files

In our HTML file, we suggested loading the file `sencha-touch-debug.js` via the script tag. You should definitely change this to `sencha-touch.js`, in order to reduce load times and memory use. You may also have used the `sencha-touch-debug.css` file to help with writing your own custom CSS. This should be changed back to `sencha-touch.css` as well.

Remove debugging code

You should also go through your application's JavaScript code and remove any `console.log` lines, alerts, or any other code you added to help you debug errors. Many mobile devices don't understand debugging code, and those that do may behave strangely if you leave it in place.

> Be sure to test out your application again once you've removed the debugging code, just to make sure you didn't delete any other code by accident.

Going that extra mile

There are some optional steps you could take before putting your application into production. With an application as simple as this one, these additional steps aren't really necessary. With larger applications, however, they can help to speed up your application and reduce its download size:

1. Minimize your JavaScript and CSS via a tool, such as YUI Compressor (http://developer.yahoo.com/yui/compressor/) or Google's Minify (http://code.google.com/p/minify/), to reduce file size.

2. Combine your separate graphics files into sprites to reduce load time.

The following are tools that can help you create sprites from your image files:

- SpriteMe - `http://spriteme.org/`
- CSS Sprite Creator - `http://www.floweringmind.com/sprite-creator/`

3. Prepare your application icon: create a 72px x 72px PNG file. Add the following to the `<head>` element of your `index.html` file: `<link rel="apple-touch-icon" href="icon.png"/>`.

Apple has a document explaining the guidelines for creating icons for your application, at `http://developer.apple.com/library/ios/#documentation/userexperience/conceptual/mobilehig/IconsImages/IconsImages.html`.

Putting the application into production

Now that you've written and tested your application, and prepared it for production, it's time to find somewhere for it to live. Since the method for putting an application into production will vary based on your setup, we will be covering this task in very general terms.

The first thing to do is to familiarize yourself with three basic pieces of the puzzle for putting your application into production: **web hosting**, **file transfer**, and **folder structure**.

While it is fine to develop your application on a local web server, if you want anyone else to see it, you will need a publically accessible web server with a constant connection to the Internet. There are a large number of web hosting providers, such as *GoDaddy*, *HostGator*, *Blue Host*, *HostMonsteror*, and *RackSpace*.

Since our application is pure HTML/JavaScript/CSS, you don't need any fancy add-ons, such as, databases or server side programming languages (PHP or Java), for your web hosting account. Any account that can serve up HTML pages is good enough. The key to this decision should be customer support. Make sure to check the reviews before choosing a provider.

The hosting provider will also supply information on setting up your domain and uploading your files to the web server. Be sure to keep good track of your username and password, for future reference.

In order to copy your application to your web hosting account, you'll probably have to familiarize yourself with a **FTP (File Transfer Protocol)** program such as **FileZilla**. As with hosting providers, there is a huge selection of FTP programs. Most of them follow a few basic conventions.

To begin with, you will need to connect to the web server with the FTP program. You will need:

- A name or IP address for the web server
- Your web hosting username and password
- A connection port for the web server

Your web hosting provider should provide you with this information when you sign up.

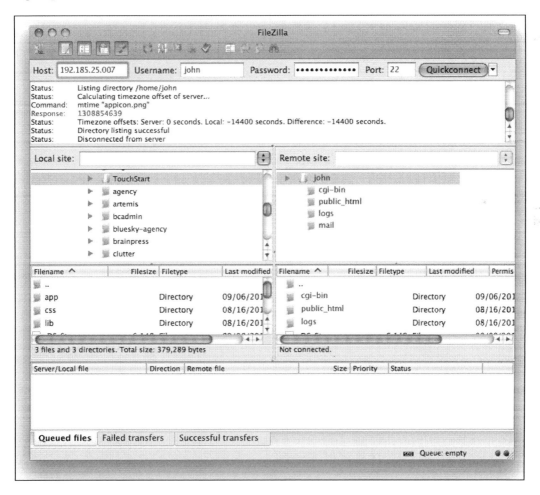

Once you are connected to the server, you will see a list of files on your local machine, and files on your remote web server. You will need to move the **TouchStart** files on the remote server to upload them. Your hosting provider will also provide you with the name of a specific folder where these files need to go. The folder is typically called something like **httpd**, **htdocs**, **html**, or **public_html**.

This brings us to our last consideration for uploading files: folder path.

The folder path affects how the application locates its files and resources. When you upload the application to the remote web server, it can affect how your folder is seen within the application. If you have any files referenced from an absolute path, such as `http://127.0.0.1/~12ftguru/TouchStart/myfile.js`, then the file will not work when you move things over to the web server.

Even relative URLs can become problematic when you transfer files to the remote server. For example, if you have a file which uses the path `/TouchStart/myFile.js`, and you upload the contents of the `TouchStart` folder instead of the folder itself, the file path will be incorrect.

This is something to keep in mind if you find yourself with missing images or other errors.

Again, your web hosting provider is your best resource for information. Be sure to look for *Getting Started* documentation and don't be afraid to seek help from any user forums that your hosting provider may have.

Summary

In this chapter, we created our first simple application. We showed some of the basics of Sencha Touch components, including configuration and nesting of components within one another. We discussed the differences between `panel` and `container` components, and when to prefer one over the other; we also introduced you to the `TabPanel` and `list` components. In addition, we explained some basic debugging methodology and prepared our application for production.

In the next chapter, we will create a custom theme for our application through the use of SASS and the Sencha Touch library's styling tools.

3

Styling the User Interface

Now that we have a basic application to build on, we are going to take a look at some of the different visual elements you can use to customize your application. In this chapter, we will:

- Take a closer look at toolbars and buttons, using layout, additional style, and icons, to boost the visual appeal of the user interface

- Expand on our previous work with icons, including making your own custom icons and using base64 to include icons in a stylesheet, without an actual image file

- Talk about the considerations and shortcuts for working with different devices and screen sizes

- Explore the incredibly powerful Sencha theme engine using SASS and Compass to create complex visual skins using simple CSS style commands

Styling components versus themes

Before we get into this chapter, it's important to have a good understanding of the difference between styling an individual component and creating a theme.

Almost every display component in Sencha Touch has an option to set its own style. For example, a `panel` component can use a style in this way:

```
{
xtype: 'panel',
style: 'border: none; font: 12px Arial black',
html: 'Hello World'
}
```

We can also set a style class for a component and use an external CSS file to define the class, as follows:

```
{
xtype: 'panel',
cls: 'myStyle',
html: 'Hello World'
}
```

These are very useful options for controlling the display of individual components. There are also certain style elements, such as border, padding, and margin, that can be set directly in the components' configuration:

```
{
xtype: 'panel',
bodyMargin: '10 5 5 5',
bodyBorder: '1px solid black',
bodyPadding: 5,
html: 'Hello World'
}
```

These configurations can accept either a number to be applied to all sides or a CSS string value, such as, 1pxsolidblack or 10555. The number should be entered without quotes, but the CSS string values need to be within quotes.

These kinds of small changes can be helpful in styling your application, but what if you need to do something a bit bigger? What if you want to change the color or appearance of the entire application? What if you want to create your own default style for your buttons?

This is where themes and UI styles come into play. We will start by taking a look at the UI styles and then see how we can expand this concept to create an overall theme for our applications.

UI styling for toolbars and buttons

Let's take another look at the simple application we created in the previous chapter and use it to start our exploration of styles with toolbars and buttons.

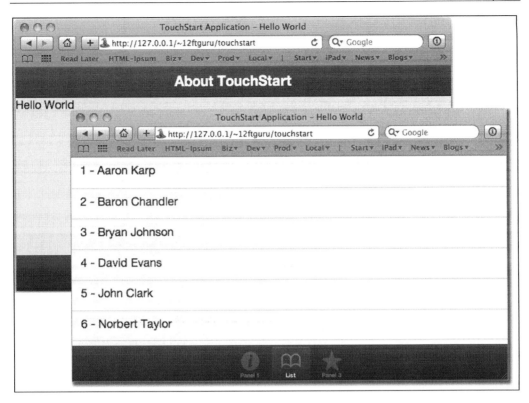

To begin our exploration of styling, we are going to add a second upper toolbar to our application. Locate the `dockedItems` section of our code from the previous example:

```
dockedItems: [
{
dock: 'top',
xtype: 'toolbar',
title: 'About TouchStart'
}
]
```

After the trailing curly brace for our first toolbar, let's add a second toolbar as follows:

```
{
dock: 'top',
xtype: 'toolbar',
title: 'About TouchStart'
}, {
```

```
dock: 'top',
xtype: 'toolbar',
items: [
{text: 'My Button'}
]
}
```

Don't forget to add a comma between the two toolbars.

Extra or missing commas

When working in Sencha Touch, one of the most common causes of parse errors is an extra or missing comma. When you are moving code around, always make sure you have accounted for any stray or missing commas. Fortunately for us, the Safari Error Console will usually give us a pretty good idea which line number to look at for these types of parse errors.

When you take a look at the new toolbar, you will see that, as it has no title, it is a bit shorter than the one above it. The title makes the top bar appear a bit bigger than the other toolbar. You can control the height of the toolbar by adding a `height` configuration to the toolbar, as follows:

```
{
dock: 'top',
xtype: 'toolbar',
height: 25,
items: [
{text: 'My Button'}
]
}
```

The `height` configuration takes a number (without quotes) to determine the height of the toolbar. You can adjust this number to fit your preference.

The two toolbars, together, also appear a bit dark, so we are going to change the appearance of the bottom bar using the `ui` configuration option:

```
{
dock: 'top',
xtype: 'toolbar',
ui: 'light',
items: [
{text: 'My Button'}
]
}
```

There are two initial values for a toolbar UI: `dark` and `light`. `dark` is the default value (used by the upper toolbar). When you save and reload the page in Safari, you should see some contrast between the upper and lower toolbars.

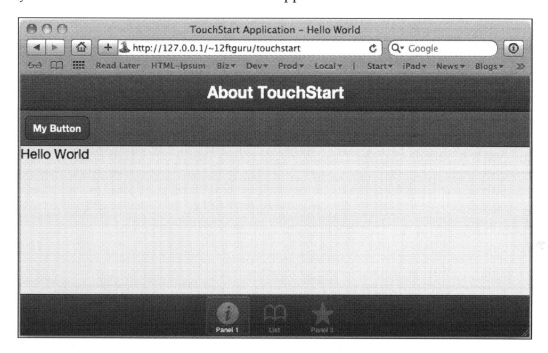

Styling buttons

Buttons also have a `ui` configuration setting, but they have different options:

- `normal`: The default button
- `back`: A button with the left side narrowed to a point
- `round`: A more drastically rounded button
- `small`: A smaller button
- `action`: A brighter version of the default button
- `forward`: A button with the right side narrowed to a point

Buttons also have some color options built into the `ui` option. These color options are `confirm` and `decline`. These options are combined with the previous shape options using a hyphen. For example, `confirm-small` or `decline-round`.

Let's add some new buttons and see how this looks. Locate the `items` list with our button, in the second toolbar:

```
items: [
  {text: 'My Button'}
]
```

Replace that old `items` list with the following new `items` list:

```
items: [
  {
text: 'Back',
ui: 'back'
  }, {
text: 'Round',
ui: 'round'
  }, {
text: 'Small',
ui: 'small'
  }, {
text: 'Normal',
ui: 'normal'
  }, {
text: 'Action',
ui: 'action'
  }, {
text: 'Forward',
ui: 'forward'
  }
]
```

As buttons can actually be used anywhere, let's also add some to the `panel` container, so we can see what the `ui` options, `confirm` and `decline`, look like. Locate the following line in our first panel:

```
html: '<div id="hello">Hello World</div>',
```

Below that line, add the following:

```
items: [
  {
xtype: 'button',
text: 'Confirm',
ui: 'confirm',
width: 100
  }, {
```

```
xtype: 'button',
text: 'Decline',
ui: 'decline',
width: 100
    }
],
```

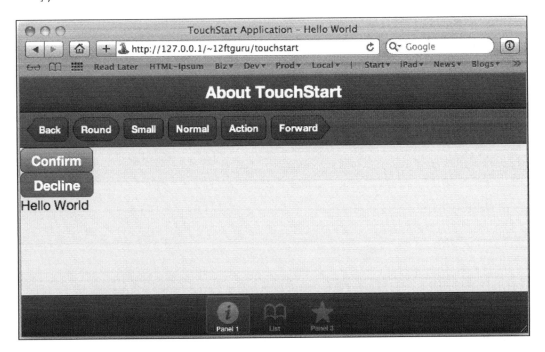

There are two things you might notice in our panel buttons that differ from our toolbar buttons. The first is that we declare `xtype: 'button'` in our panel, but we don't in our toolbar. This is because the toolbar assumes it will contain buttons, and `xtype` only has to be declared if you use something other than a button. The panel does not set default `xtype` attribute, so every item in the panel must declare one.

The second difference is that we declare `width` for the buttons. If we don't declare `width` when we use a button in a panel, it will expand to the full width of the panel. On the toolbar, the button auto-sizes itself to fit the text.

These simple styling options can help make your application easier to navigate and provide the user with visual clues for important or potentially destructive actions.

The tab bar

Like the toolbar, the tab bar at the bottom also understands the `ui` configuration option for both `light` and `dark`. However, the tab bar also changes the icon appearance, based on the `ui` option; a `light` toolbar will have dark icons and a `dark` toolbar will have light icons.

These icons are actually black-and-white images that are used to create a mask over the color of the tab bar. Later in the chapter, we will show you how to create your own icon masks and integrate them into your application.

While we are on the subject of icons, we should also take a look at the basic icons you will want to include with your application.

Sencha Touch themes

Themes in Sencha Touch are a powerful way to quickly change the overall look and feel of your application. We will cover the installation process a bit later in this chapter, but we do need to lay a bit of groundwork before we can get started. There is a lot of conceptual information to cover, but the flexibility you gain will be well worth the effort.

The first thing we need to cover is a basic overview of the tools used by Sencha Touch that make theming your application possible: SASS and Compass.

 If you are already familiar with SASS and Compass, or you are more comfortable installing first and then covering the concepts, you can skip ahead to the *Setting up SASS and Compass* section.

An introduction to SASS and Compass

SASS stands for **Syntactically Awesome Stylesheets**, and it's used to extend standard CSS to allow for variables, nesting, mixins, and selector inheritance. This means that all of your regular CSS declarations will work just fine, but you also get some extra goodies.

Variables in SASS

Variables allow you to define specific values and then use them throughout the stylesheet. Variables' names are arbitrary and start with a $. For example, we can use SASS to define the following:

```
$blue: #4D74C1;
$red: #800000;
$baseMargin: 10px;
$basePadding: 5px;
```

We can then use these variables as part of our standard CSS declarations in the SASS file:

```
.box1 {
border: 1px solid $blue;
padding: $basePadding;
margin: $baseMargin;
}
```

We can also use basic math functions, as follows:

```
.box2 {
border: 1px solid $blue;
padding: $basePadding * 2;
margin: $baseMargin / 2;
}
```

This creates a box with twice the padding and half the margin of the first box. This is great for creating flexible, scalable layouts. By changing your base values, you can quickly scale your application to deal with multiple devices, with multiple resolutions and screen sizes.

Additionally, when you decide you want to change the shade of blue you are using, you only have to change it in one place. SASS also has a number of built-in functions for adjusting colors, such as:

- `darken`: Makes the color darker by percentage
- `lighten`: Makes the color lighter by percentage
- `complement`: Returns the complementary color
- `invert`: Returns the inverted color
- `saturate`: Saturates the color by a numerical amount
- `desaturate`: Desaturates the color by a numerical amount

These functions allow you to do things such as the following:

```
.pullQuote {
border: 1px solid blue;
color: darken($blue, 15%);
}
```

There are also functions for numbers, lists, strings, and basic if-then statements. These functions help make your stylesheet every bit as flexible as your programming code.

SASS functions

The full list of SASS functions can be found at `http://sass-lang.com/docs/yardoc/Sass/Script/Functions.html`.

Mixins in SASS

Mixins are a variation of the standard SASS variables. Avoid simply declaring a single one-to-one variable, such as the following:

```
$margin: 10px;
```

Instead, you can use a mixin to declare an entire CSS class as a variable:

```
@mixinbaseDiv {
border: 1px solid #f00;
color: #333;
width: 200px;
}
```

You can then take that mixin and use it in the SASS file:

```
#specificDiv {
padding: 10px;
margin: 10px;
float: right;
@includebaseDiv;
}
```

This gives you all of the attributes of the `baseDivmixin` component, plus the specific styles you declared in the `#specificDiv` class.

You can also set your mixin to use arguments, to make it even more flexible. Let's look at an alternative version of what we had previously:

```
@mixinbaseDiv($width, $margin, $float) {
border: 1px solid #f00;
color: #333;
width: $width;
margin: $margin;
float: $float;
}
```

This means we can set values for width, margin, and float, as part of our SASS code, such as the following:

```
#divLeftSmall {
@includebaseDiv(100px, 10px, left);
}
#divLeftBig{
@includebaseDiv(300px, 10px, left);
}
#divRightBig {
@includebaseDiv(300px, 10px, right);
}
#divRightAlert {
@includebaseDiv(100px, 10px, right);
color: #F00;
font-weight: bold;
}
```

This gives us four `div` tags with slightly different properties. All of them share the same base properties of the `mixinbaseDiv` class, but they have different values for `width` and `float`. We can also override the values for `mixinbaseDiv`, by adding them in after we include the mixin, as seen in our `#divRightAlert` example.

Nesting in SASS

SASS also allows nesting of CSS declarations. This not only lets you write styles that more closely mirror the structure of your HTML, but also makes for cleaner, more easily maintainable code.

In HTML, we often nest elements within one another to give the document a structure. A common example of this would be an unordered list that contains several list items, such as the following:

```
<ul>
<li>Main List Item 1</li>
<li>Main List Item 2</li>
</ul>
```

Normally, to style this list via CSS, you would write rules for the ul elements, separately from the rules for the li elements. The two rules might not even be near one another in your CSS files, making debugging or modifying the styles more difficult.

In SASS, we can write the following:

```
ul {
width: 150px;
border: 1px solid red;

li {
margin: 1px;
border: 1px solid blue;
}


}
```

See how we nest the style declarations for our li element inside the style declaration for ul? Not only does this match the structure of the HTML document, but when you want to update the li element, you know that it can be found inside the ul element.

When you compile that with SASS, the resulting CSS has separate rules for the ul and li elements:

```
ul {
width: 150px;
border: 1px solid red;
}
ul li {
margin: 1px;
border: 1px solid blue;
}
```

If you were to view this list in your browser, you would see a list with a red border around it, and blue borders around each of the individual list items.

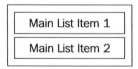

It's also possible to reference the item one level up in the nesting, via the ampersand (&) character. This is useful when adding things like hover states to nested elements, or more generally, keeping exceptions to your rules grouped together.

Suppose we want to change the background color when we hover over one of our li elements. We could add `&:hover` inside the li style declaration:

```
ul {
width: 150px;
border: 1px solid red;

li {
margin: 1px;
border: 1px solid blue;

&:hover {
background-color: #B3C6FF;
}

}

}
```

The `&:hover` gets translated into `li:hover` by the SASS compiler:

```
ulli:hover {
background-color: #B3C6FF;
}
```

The `&` special character doesn't have to be used at the beginning of a rule, either. Say your designer has your li elements use a bigger border when they're located in a special `#sidebardiv` component. You could write a separate rule after your ul/li rules, or you could add the exception inside the li ruleset, using the special `&` character:

```
ul {
li {
margin: 1px;
border: 1px solid blue;

&:hover {
background-color: #B3C6FF;
}
div#sidebar& {
border-width: 3px;
}
}
}
```

This will be translated to the following rule:

```
div#sidebarul li { border-width: 3px; }
```

You can also nest CSS namespaces. In CSS, if properties all start with the same prefix, such as `font-`, then you can nest them as well:

```
li {
font: {
family: Verdana;
size: 18px;
weight: bold;
}
}
```

Be sure to remember to put the colon after the namespace name. When compiled, this will become the following:

```
li {
font-family: Verdana;
font-size: 18px;
font-weight: bold;
}
```

This works for any namespace CSS property, such as, `border-` or `background-`.

Selector inheritance in SASS

Selector inheritance in SASS is analogous to object inheritance in JavaScript. In the same way, a `panel` component extends the `container` object, meaning that a `panel` has all the properties and functions of a `container`, and then some. SASS lets you have objects that inherit the styles of other objects.

Say we want to create some message box elements for our application, one for informational messages and one for errors. First, we should define a generic box:

```
.messageBox {
margin: 10px;
width: 150px;
border: 1px solid;
font: {
size: 24px;
weight: bold;
}
}
```

Now, in any class where we want to include the `.messageBox` styles, we just use the `@extend` directive `@extend.messageBox;`, on a line by itself:

```
.errorBox {
@extend .messageBox;
border-color: red;
color: red;
}

.infoBox {
@extend .messageBox;
border-color: blue;
color: blue;
}
```

Then, in our HTML, we would just use the `.errorBox` and `.infoBox` classes:

```
<div class="infoBox">Here's some information you may like to have.</
div>
<div class="errorBox">An unspecified error has occurred.</div>
```

Put it all together and you will see the left box with a blue border and blue text. The right box will have a red border and red text:

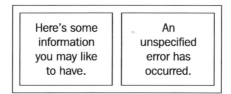

Compass

Just as Sencha Touch is a framework built on the lower-level languages of JavaScript, CSS, and HTML, Compass is a framework built on SASS and CSS. Compass provides a suite of reusable components for styling your application, such as:

- **CSS Resets**, which enforce a uniform appearance for most HTML across all of the major web browsers.

- **Mixins**, which allow you to declare complex programmatic functions for your CSS.

- **Layouts and Grids**, which enforce width and height standards, to assist in keeping your layout consistent across all pages.

- **Image Spriting**, which allows you to automatically generate a single image from multiple smaller images (this is easier for the browser to download). The CSS will automatically show just the portion of the image you need, hiding the rest.

- **Text Replacement**, which allows you to automatically swap specific text pieces within your document.

- **Typography**, which provides advanced options for using fonts within your web pages.

Compass also incorporates, into its components, the latest in CSS best practices, meaning that your stylesheet will be leaner and more efficient.

SASS + Compass = themes

Sencha Touch themes take SASS and Compass one step further, by providing variables and mixins whose functionality is specific to Sencha Touch. The JavaScript portion of Sencha Touch generates lots of very complex HTML, in order to display the various components, such as toolbars and panels. Rather than having to learn all of the intricate classes and HTML tricks used by Sencha Touch, you can simply use the appropriate mixins to change the appearance of your application.

Setting up SASS and Compass

If you decide that you would like to create your own Sencha Touch theme, you will have to install both SASS and Compass, which are separate libraries from Sencha Touch.

Installing SASS and Compass requires us to do a bit of work on the command line. Since both SASS and Compass are available as **RubyGems**, Windows users will first need to install **Ruby**.

Installing Ruby

Mac users get a break, since Ruby is already installed on OSX by default. Windows users should download the Ruby installer from `http://rubyinstaller.org/`. (We recommend version 1.9.2.)

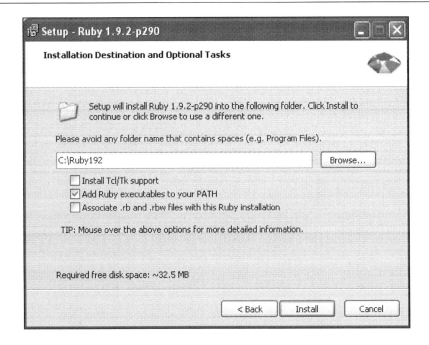

Run the installer and follow the onscreen instructions to install Ruby. Be sure to check the box that says **Add Ruby executables to your PATH**. This will save you a lot of typing on the command line, later on.

Once the installation is complete, open up the command line in Windows by going to **Start | Run**, typing **cmd**, and pressing *Enter*. This should bring up the command line.

Now, try typing **ruby -v**. You should see something such as the following:

```
C:\Ruby192>ruby -v
ruby 1.9.2p180 (2011-02-18) [i386-mingw32]
```

This means that Ruby is correctly installed.

Installing SASS and Compass

The instructions for installing SASS and Compass vary slightly for Mac and Windows users.

Mac users will need to open the Terminal application and type the following:

```
sudo gem install haml
sudo gem install compass
```

You will need to authenticate with your username and password to complete the install.

Windows users need to open the command line and type the following:

```
gem install haml
gem install compass
```

Once the installation is complete, we are ready to set up our folders and begin using SASS and Compass.

If you're not comfortable with this command line stuff, there are two applications that bundle up Ruby, SASS, and Compass for you, and run on both Windows and OSX:

- Scout: http://mhs.github.com/scout-app/
- Compass.app: http://compass.handlino.com/

Creating a custom theme

The next thing we need to do is create our own theme SCSS file. Locate the sencha-touch.scss file in **TouchStart/lib/resources/sass**, and make a copy of the file. Rename the new copy of the file to **myTheme.scss**.

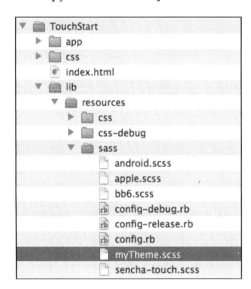

Now, we need to tell the index to look for our new theme. Using our previous example files, open your `index.html` file, and locate the line that says the following:

```
<link rel="stylesheet" href="lib/resources/css/sencha-touch.css"
type="text/css">
```

Change the `sencha-touch.css` stylesheet reference in our `index.html` file to point to `myTheme.css`:

```
<link rel="stylesheet" href="lib/resources/css/myTheme.css"
type="text/css">
```

SCSS and CSS

Notice that we are currently including a stylesheet from the `css` folder, called `sencha-touch.css`, and we have a matching file in the `scss` folder, called `sencha-touch.scss`. When the SCSS files are compiled, it creates a new file in your `css` folder. This new file will have a suffix of `.css` instead of `.scss`.

`.scss` is the file extension for SASS files. **SCSS** is short for **Sassy CSS**.

Now that we have our paths set up, let's take a look at the theme file copy we made. Open your `myTheme.scss` file. You should see the following:

```
@import 'sencha-touch/default/all';

@includesencha-panel;
@includesencha-buttons;
@includesencha-sheet;
@includesencha-picker;
@includesencha-tabs;
@includesencha-toolbar;
@includesencha-toolbar-forms;
@includesencha-carousel;
@includesencha-indexbar;
@includesencha-list;
@includesencha-list-paging
@includesencha-list-pullrefresh;
@includesencha-layout;
@includesencha-form;
@includesencha-msgbox;
@includesencha-loading-spinner;
```

This code grabs all of the default Sencha Touch theme files and compiles them into a new CSS file located in the css folder. If you open up the `sencha-touch.css` file in the `lib/resources/css` folder, you will see the compressed CSS file we were previously using. This file is pretty huge, but it's all created from the basic commands.

The best part is that we can now change the entire color scheme of the application with a single line of code.

Base color

One of the key variables in the Sencha Touch theme is `$base_color`. This color and its variations are used throughout the entire theme. To see what we mean, let's change the color of our theme to a nice forest green by adding the following to the top of your `myTheme.scss` file (above all the other text):

```
$base_color: #546346;
```

Next, we need to re-compile the SASS file to create our stylesheet. From the command line, you need to change into the `sass` folder where your `myTheme.scss` file lives. Once you are in the folder, type the following into the command line and hit *Enter*:

```
compass compile
```

This will update our `myTheme.css` file with the new `$base_color` value. Reload the page in Safari, and you should see a new forest green look to your application.

Notice that this one line of code has created variations for both our dark and light toolbars. Changing the base color has also changed the icons for our tab bar at the bottom.

This is all pretty cool, but what if we want to tweak individual parts of the theme? Sencha Touch themes provides exactly what we need, using mixins and the `ui` configuration option.

compass compile **versus** compass watch

Compass uses the `compile` command to create the new stylesheet, based on your SCSS file. However, you can also set Compass up to watch a particular file for changes and automatically compile when anything new is added. This command is entered on the command line as the following:

compass watch filename

This command will remain active as long as your terminal is open. Once you close the terminal window, you will need to run the command again, in order to make Compass watch for changes.

Mixins and the UI configuration

As we have noted previously, the Sencha theme system is a set of predefined mixins and variables that get compiled to create a CSS stylesheet. Each component has its own mixins and variables for controlling styles. This means you can override these variables or use the mixins to customize your own theme.

You can also use mixins to create additional options for the `ui` configuration option (beyond the simple `light` and `dark` values that we have seen previously). For example, we can modify the color of our toolbar by adding a new mixin to our `myTheme.sass` file.

In your `myTheme.sass` file, locate the line that says the following:

```
@import 'sencha-touch/default/all';
```

After that line, add the following:

```
@includesencha-toolbar-ui('subnav', #625546, 'matte');
```

This code tells SASS to create a new `ui` option for the toolbar. Our new option will be called `subnav`, and it will have a base color of `#625546`. The last option sets the style for the gradient. The available styles are:

- `flat`: No gradient
- `matte`: A subtle gradient
- `bevel`: A medium gradient
- `glossy`: A glassy style gradient
- `recessed`: A reversed gradient

Once you have saved the file, you will need to recompile the stylesheet, using the `compass compile` command on the command line.

We also need to change the `ui` configuration option in our JavaScript file. Locate your `touchStart.js` file in the `app` folder and open it up. Find the second toolbar in our application, just above where we add the buttons. It should look like the following:

```
dock: 'top',
xtype: 'toolbar',
ui: 'light'
```

You will need to change `ui:'light'` to `ui:'subnav'` and save the file.

You can then reload the page to see your changes.

Adding new icon masks

You can also use the mixins to add custom icon masks to your tab bar at the bottom, using the `pictos-iconmaskmixin` component. There are two caveats to keep in mind when using this function.

The first is that these icons are used as a mask for the button. This means that the icon is a transparent PNG file that only uses the color black. This icon is then used to screen a particular color by allowing it to show through any of the black areas. For example, the actual PNG file for our info mask is on the far left in the following screenshot. Depending on the `ui` configuration for the tab, it can appear in a number of different colors, also shown as follows:

The original PNG file is also larger than our theme items, which allows the file to be scaled to fit a number of different sizes.

The second consideration for using the `pictos-iconmaskmixin` component is that it expects the icon file to be in a specific folder: `/lib/resources/themes/images/default/pictos`. If you open this folder, you will see that there are already a number of extra icons in the folder.

For example, we have an icon called "bolt", but if we try to use it as part of our `touchStart.js` file, we end up with a blank square instead of the icon. We need to use our mixin to actually add it to our SCSS and CSS files.

In your `myTheme.sass` file, locate the line that says:

```
@import 'sencha-touch/default/all';
```

After that line, add the following:

```
@includepictos-iconmask('bolt');
```

In this case, we are telling the mixin to include an icon mask for the `bolt.png` icon file. The argument for the mixin is always the name of the file without the `.png` extension. This is also the name we will use to add the icon to our JavaScript file.

In the `touchStart.js` file, locate the line that says:

```
iconCls: 'info',
```

Replace the line with the following:

```
iconCls: 'bolt',
```

Save your changes and reload the page to see your new icon. Don't forget to recompile the SASS file using `compass compile` on the command line.

You can also add your own custom mask files to this folder and call them, using the same `pictos-iconmaskmixin` function in your SASS file, and adding the corresponding `iconCls` configuration option to your `js` file. Just make sure they are transparent PNG files with black icons, and that you put them in the correct folder, that is, `/lib/resources/themes/images/default/pictos`.

Variables

Variables are also available for every component, and they are used to control specific color, size, and appearance options. Unlike mixins, the variables target a single setting for a component. For example, the `button` component includes variables for the following:

- `$button-gradient`: The default gradient for all buttons
- `$button-height`: The default height for all buttons
- `$button-radius`: The default border radius for all buttons
- `$button-stroke-weight`: The default border thickness for all buttons

There are also variables for disabling all of the special CSS effects on all buttons (gradients, text shadows, and drop shadows) as well as setting the default size for toolbar icons.

For example, if we add `$button-height: 2em;` to our `myTheme.scss` file, then we can recompile and see that buttons in our toolbar are now larger than they were before.

You will also notice that our **Confirm** and **Decline** buttons did not change size. This is because their UI configurations (confirm and decline) have already been defined separately and include a specific height. If you wanted to change the size of these two buttons, you would need to remove the UI configuration for both buttons.

More SASS resources

Using the mixins and variables included in the Sencha Touch theme, you can change almost any aspect of your interface to look exactly how you want. There are a number of online resources that will help you dig deeper into all of the possibilities with SASS and Compass.

Additional resources

- A full list of the Sencha Touch theme mixins and variables is available at http://dev.sencha.com/deploy/touch/docs/theme/
- Learn more about SASS at http://sass-lang.com/
- The Compass home page has examples of sites using Compass, tutorials, help, and more, at http://compass-style.org/

Designing for multiple devices

When creating stylesheets for your application, it's also important to consider the appearance of your application on multiple devices. Each device will have its own screen size, which limits the available area of your application.

What we really need is a way to determine the type of device we are on. We can accomplish this by using the Sencha Touch is function. The is function simply returns true or false for the following arguments:

- Android
- Blackberry
- Desktop
- Linux
- Mac
- Phone
- Tablet
- Windows

- iOS
- iPad
- iPhone
- iPod

You can also use standalone to detect if the application has been saved to the home screen. For example, if you want check screen sizes, you can use something such as the following:

```
if(Ext.is.Tablet || Ext.is.Desktop) {
// use full size elements here
} else {
// use phone size elements here
}
```

Basically, this code checks if the application is running on either a tablet or desktop. If it is, we can then add code to create our full-sized interface. If is not running on either of these two device types, we can create a smaller interface for phones, iPods, and other smaller devices.

You can use these tests to resize your various components and change styles, based on the device the application is running on. Here's an example:

```
if(Ext.is.Tablet || Ext.is.Desktop) {
  varfontSize = '12px';
  vardefaultUI = 'normal';
  varbuttonWidth = 100;
} else {
  varfontSize = '16px';
  vardefaultUI = 'large';
  varbuttonWidth = 200;
}


newExt.Application({
name: 'TouchStart',
launch: function() {
var about = new Ext.Panel({
fullscreen: true,
title: 'Touch Start',
html: 'Changing type sizes based on the device',
style: 'font-size: '+fontSize+';',
items: [{
xtype: 'button',
text: 'My button',
ui: defaultUI,
width: buttonWidth
```

```
                }]
        });

    this.viewport = about;
        }
    });
```

This example code first checks to see if we are running on a tablet or a desktop machine. If we are running on one of those two environments, we make our `font-size`, `defaultUI`, and `buttonWidth` configuration options a default size.

If we are running on any other type of device (something with a small screen), we make the font size and component sizes a bit larger to aid with visibility and interaction.

Our application code then sets up a single panel with a button, both of which use the size values we defined in the previous example.

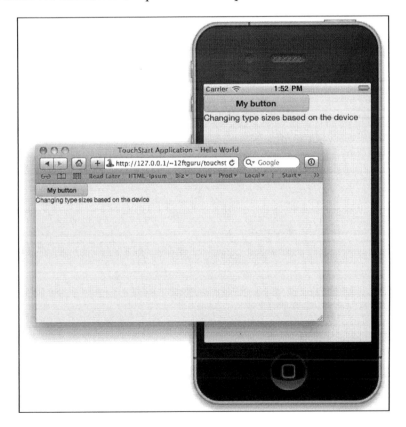

These types of conditional style tweaks will help keep your application readable and usable across multiple devices.

Images on multiple devices with Sencha.io Src

If your application uses images, you probably need something a bit more robust than conditional styles, such as those used in the previous section. Creating individual image sets for each device would be a nightmare. Fortunately, the folks at Sencha have an answer to this problem: a web-based service called `Sencha.io Src`.

`Sencha.io Src` is a separate service from Sencha Touch and can be used in any web-based application. The service works by taking an original image and resizing it on the fly, to fit the current device and screen size. These images are also cached by the service and optimized for quick, repeatable delivery. To use the `Sencha.io Src` service, the only thing you need to change is the URL for your image.

For example, a basic HTML image tag looks like this:

```
<img src="http://www.mydomain.com/images/my-big-image.jpg">
```

The same image tag, using the `Sencha.io Src` service, would look like this:

```
<img src="http://src.sencha.io/http://www.mydomain.com/images/my-big-
image.jpg">
```

This passes the actual URL of your image to the system for processing.

Image URLs in Sencha.io Src

As you can see in the example, we are using a full image URL (with `http://www.mydomain.com/`), instead of a shorter relative URL (such as `/images/my-big-image.jpg`). Since the `Sencha.io Src` service needs to be able to get directly to the file from the main `Sencha.io` server, a relative URL will not work. The image file needs to be on a publicly available web server in order to work correctly.

By using the service, our large image will be scaled to fit the full width of our device's screen, no matter what size device we use. Sencha.io Src also keeps the image proportions correct, without any squishing or stretching.

Specifying sizes with Sencha.io Src

We don't always use fullscreen images in our applications. We often use them for things such as icons and accents, within the application. Sencha.io Src also lets us specify a particular height and/or width for an image:

```
<img src="http://src.sencha.io/320/200/http://www.mydomain.com/images/
my-big-image.jpg">
```

In this case, we have set the width of our image to be resized to 320 pixels, and the height to 200 pixels. We can also constrain just the width, and the height will automatically be set to the correct proportion:

```
<img src="http://src.sencha.io/320/http://www.mydomain.com/images/my-
big-image.jpg">
```

It is important to note that Sencha.io Src will only shrink images. It will not enlarge them. If you enter a value larger than the dimensions of the actual image, it will simply display at the full image size.

You full-size image should always be the largest size you will need for display.

Sizing by formula

We can also use formulas to make changes based on the screen size of the device. For example, we can use the following code to make our photo 20 pixels narrower than the full width of the screen:

```
<img src="http://src.sencha.io/-20/http://www.mydomain.com/images/my-
big-image.jpg">
```

This is useful if you want to leave a small border around the image.

Sizing by percentage

We can also use percentage widths to set our image sizes:

```
<img src="http://src.sencha.io/x50/http://www.mydomain.com/images/my-
big-image.jpg">
```

The x50 part of our URL sets the image size to 50 percent of the screen width.

We can even combine these two elements to create a scalable image gallery:

```
<img src="http://src.sencha.io/-20x50-5/http://www.mydomain.com/
images/my-big-image.jpg">
<img src="http://src.sencha.io/-20x50-5/http://www.mydomain.com/
images/my-big-image.jpg">
```

By using the formula `-20x50-5`, we take our original image, remove 20 pixels for our margin, shrink it to 50 percent, and then remove an additional five pixels, to allow for space between our two images.

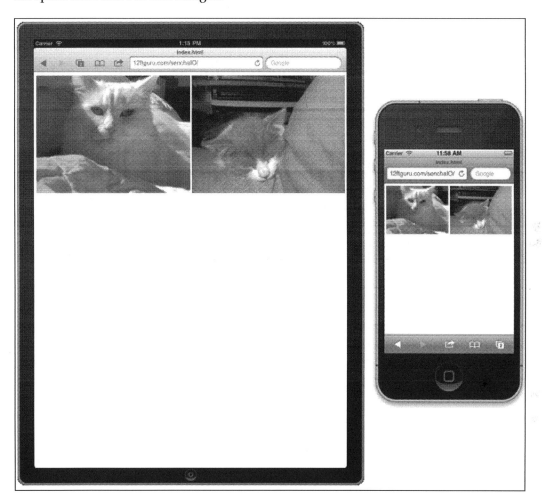

Changing file types

`Sencha.io Src` offers some additional options you might find useful. The first lets you change the file type for your image on the fly. For example, the following code will return your JPG file as a PNG:

```
<img src="http://src.sencha.io/png/http://www.mydomain.com/images/my-
big-image.jpg">
```

This can be useful when offering your applications' users multiple download options for images.

This option can also be combined with the resizing options:

```
<img src="http://src.sencha.io/png/x50/http://www.mydomain.com/images/
my-big-image.jpg">
```

This would convert the file to PNG format and scale it to 50 percent.

By using the functions available in `Sencha.io Src`, you can automatically size images for your application and provide a consistent look and feel across multiple devices.

For a full list of all the functions you can use with `Sencha.io Src`, go to `http://www.sencha.com/learn/how-to-use-src-sencha-io/`.

Summary

In this chapter, we covered how to style toolbars using the `ui` configuration option. We also talked about how Sencha Touch uses SASS and Compass to create a robust theme system. We included installation instructions for SASS and Compass and provided an explanation of mixins, variables, nesting, and selector inheritance. Finally, we touched upon designing interfaces for multiple devices and handling automatic image resizing, using `Sencha.io Src`.

In the next chapter, we will dive right back into the Sencha Touch framework. We'll review a bit of what we have previously learned about component hierarchy. Then, we will cover some of the more specialized components that are available. Finally, we'll give you some tips on finding the information you need in the Sencha Touch API documentation.

4
Components and Configurations

In this chapter, we are going to take a deeper look at the individual components available in Sencha Touch. We will examine the layout configuration option and how it affects each of the components.

Throughout the chapter, we will use the simple base components as a starting point for learning about the more complex components. We'll also talk a bit about how to access our components after they have been created.

Finally, we will wrap up with a look at how to use the Sencha Touch API documentation to find detailed information on configurations, properties, methods, and events for each component.

This chapter will cover the following topics:

- The base component class
- Layouts revisited
- The TabPanel and Carousel components
- The FormPanel components
- MessageBox and Sheet
- The map component
- The List and NestedList components
- Where to find more information on components

The base component class

When we talk about components in Sencha Touch, we are generally talking about buttons, panels, sliders, toolbars, form fields, and other tangible items that we can see on the screen. However, all of these components inherit their configuration options, methods, properties, and events from a single base component with the startlingly original name of component. This can obviously lead to a bit of confusion, so we will refer to this as Ext.Component for the rest of this book.

One of the most important things to understand is that you will never actually use Ext.Component directly. It is simply used as a building block for all of the other components in Sencha Touch. However, it is important to be familiar with the base component class, because anything it can do, all the other components can do. Learning this one class can give you a huge head start on everything else. Some of the more useful configuration options of Ext.Component are as follows:

- border
- cls
- disabled
- height/width
- hidden
- html
- margin
- padding
- scroll
- style
- ui

Since the other components, which we will cover in this chapter, inherit from the base component class, they will all have these same configuration options.

Ext.Component also contains a number of useful methods that will allow you to get and set properties on any Sencha Touch component. Here are a few of those methods:

- addCls and removeCls: Add or remove a CSS class from your component.
- destroy: Remove the component from memory.
- disable and enable: Disable or enable the component (very useful in forms).

- `getHeight`, `getWidth`, and `getSize`: Get the current height, width, or size of the component. Size returns both height and width. You can also use `setHeight`, `setWidth`, and `setSize`, to change the dimensions of your component.

- `show` and `hide`: Show or hide the component.

- `setPosition`: Set the top and left values for the component.

- `update`: Update the content area of a component.

Unlike our configuration options, methods can only be used once the component is created. This means we also need to understand how to get the component itself before we can begin using the methods. This is where the `Ext` class comes into play.

The Ext object and Ext.getCmp()

The `Ext` object is created, by default, when the Sencha Touch library is loaded. This object has methods that are used to create our initial application and its components. It also allows us to talk to our other components after they have been created. For example, let's take the very first code example we used in *Chapter 2, Creating a Simple Application*:

```
new Ext.Application({
    name: 'TouchStart',
    launch: function() {
        var hello = new Ext.Container({
            fullscreen: true,
            html: '<div id="hello">Hello World</div>',
            id: 'helloContainer'
        });

        this.viewport = hello;
    }
});
```

Sharp-eyed readers will note that I have modified our original code a bit and added an `id` configuration option to the container. This configuration option, `id: 'helloContainer'` will allow us to grab the container, later on, using our `Ext` class and the method `getCmp()`.

For example, we can add the following code after `this.viewport = hello;`:

```
var myContainer = Ext.getCmp('helloContainer');
myContainer.update('Hello Again!');
```

By using `Ext.getCmp`, we get back the component with an `id` value of `helloContainer`, which we then set to our variable `myContainer`. Using this method returns an actual component, in this case a container.

Since we get this object back as a container component, we can use any of the methods that the container understands. For our example, we used the `update()` method to change the content of the container to `'Hello Again!'`. Typically, these types of changes will be generated by a button click and not in the launch function. This example simply shows that we can manipulate the component on the fly even after it gets created.

The ID configuration

It's a good idea to include an `id` configuration in all of your components. This makes it possible to use `Ext.getCmp()` to get to those components, later on, when we need them. Remember to keep the ID of every component unique. If you plan on creating multiple copies of a component, you will need to make sure that a unique ID is generated for each copy.

The `Ext.getCmp()` method is great for grabbing Sencha Touch components and manipulating them. We will be using this method in a few of our examples, in this chapter.

Layouts revisited

Layouts are another area we need to expand upon. When you start creating your own applications, you will need a firm understanding of how the different layouts affect what you see on the screen. To this end, we are going to start out with a demonstration application that shows how the different layouts work.

For the purposes of this demo application, we will create the different components, one at a time, as individual variables. This is done for the sake of readability and should not be considered the best programming style. Remember that any items created this way will take up memory, even if the user never views the component.

```
var myPanel = new Ext.Panel({ …
```

It is always a much better practice to create your components, using `xtype` attibutes, within your main container:

```
items: [{ xtype: 'panel', …
```

This allows Sencha Touch to render the components as they are needed, instead of all at once when the page loads.

The card layout

To begin with, we will create a simple card layout:

```
new Ext.Application({
    name: 'TouchStart',
    launch: function() {
        var layoutPanel = new Ext.Panel({
            fullscreen: true,
            layout: 'card',
        id: 'layoutPanel',
            cardSwitchAnimation: 'slide',
        items: [hboxTest]
        });

        this.viewport = layoutPanel;
    }
});
```

This sets up a single panel with a card layout. The card layout arranges its items similar to a stack of cards. Only one of these cards is active and displayed at a time. The card layout keeps any additional cards in the background and only creates them when the panel receives the `setActiveItem()` command.

Each item in the list can be activated by using `setActiveItem()` and the item number. This can be a bit confusing, as the numbering of the items is zero-indexed, meaning that you start counting at zero and not one. For example, if you want to activate the fourth item in the list, you would use:

```
layoutPanel.setActiveItem(3);
```

In this case, we are starting out with only a single card/item called `hboxTest`. We need to add this container to make our program run.

The hbox layout

Above the line that says `var layoutPanel = new Ext.Panel({`, in the preceding code, add the following code:

```
var hboxTest =   new Ext.Container({
        layout: {
            type: 'hbox',
            align: 'stretch'
        },
        items: [{
```

```
          xtype: 'container',
          flex: 1,
          html: 'My flex is 1',
          margin: 5,
          style: 'background-color: #7FADCF'
        }, {
          xtype: 'container',
          flex: 2,
          html: 'My flex is 2',
          margin: 5,
          style: 'background-color: #7FADCF'
        }, {
          xtype: 'container',
          width: 80,
          html: 'My width is 80',
          margin: 5,
          style: 'background-color: #7FADCF'
        }]
    });
```

This gives us a container with an hbox layout and three child items.

Child and parent

In Sencha Touch, we often find ourselves dealing with very large arrays of items, nested in containers that are in turn nested in other containers. It is often helpful to refer to a container as a parent to any items it contains. These items are then referred to as the children of the container.

The hbox layout stacks its items horizontally and uses the `width` and `flex` values to determine how much horizontal space each of its child items will take up. The `align: 'stretch'` configuration causes the items to stretch to fill all of the available vertical space.

If we run the code now, we should see this:

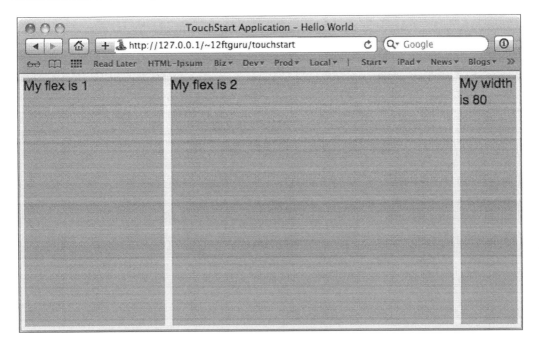

You should try adjusting the flex and width values to see how it affects the size of the child containers. You can also change the available configuration options for align (center, end, start, and stretch), to see the different options available. Once you are finished, let's move on and add some more items to our card layout.

The vbox layout

Above our previous var hboxTest = new Ext.Container({ code, add the following:

```
var vboxTest =  new Ext.Container({
        layout: {
            type: 'vbox',
            align: 'stretch'
        },
        items: [{
          xtype: 'container',
          flex: 1,
          html: 'My flex is 1',
          margin: 5,
          style: 'background-color: #7FADCF'
        }, {
```

```
        xtype: 'container',
        flex: 2,
        html: 'My flex is 2',
        margin: 5,
        style: 'background-color: #7FADCF'
    }, {
        xtype: 'container',
        height: 80,
        html: 'My height is 80',
        margin: 5,
        style: 'background-color: #7FADCF'
    }]
});
```

This code is virtually identical to our previous hbox code, a container with three child containers. However, this parent container uses layout: vbox, and the third child container in the items list uses height instead of width. This is because the vbox layout stacks its items vertically and uses the values for height and flex to determine how much space the child items will take up. In this layout, the align: 'stretch' configuration causes the items to stretch to fill the horizontal space.

Now that we have our vbox container, we need to add it to the items in our main layoutContainer. Change the items list in layoutContainer to say the following:

```
items: [hboxTest, vboxTest]
```

If we run the code now, it's going to look exactly the same as before. This is because our card layout on layoutContainer can only have one active item. You can set layoutContainer to show our new vbox by adding the following configuration to our layoutContainer:

```
activeItem: 1,
```

Remember that our items are numbered starting with zero, so item 1 is the second item in our list: items: [hboxTest, vboxTest].

You should now be able to see the vbox layout for our application:

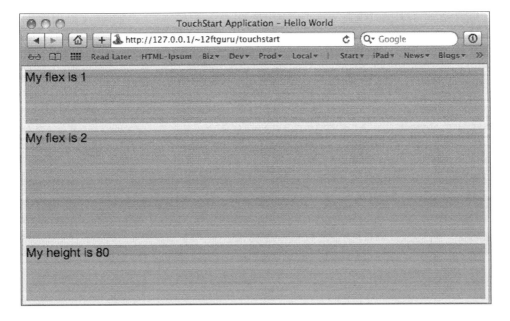

As with the hbox, you should take a moment to adjust the `flex` and `width` values and see how it affects the size of the containers. You can also change the available configuration options for `align` (`center`, `end`, `start`, and `stretch`), to see the different options available. Once you are finished, let's move on and add some more items to our card layout.

The fit layout

The fit layout is the most basic layout and it simply fits any child items to the parent container. While this seems pretty basic, it can also have some unintended consequences, as we will see in our example.

Above our preceding `var vboxTest = new Ext.Container({` code, add the following:

```
var fitTest =  new Ext.Container({
        layout: 'fit',
        items: [{
          xtype: 'button',
          ui: 'decline',
          text: 'Do Not Press'
        }]
      });
```

This is a single container with a fit layout and a button. Now, all we need to do is set the `activeItem` configuration on our main `layoutContainer` component by changing `activeItem: 1` to `activeItem: 2`.

If you reload the page now, you will see what we mean by unintended consequences:

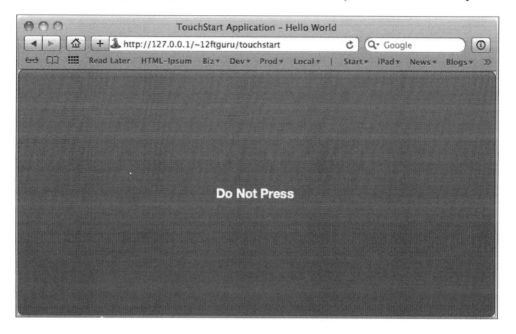

As you can see, our button has expanded to fill the entire screen. We can change this by declaring a specific height and width for the button (and any other items we place in this container). However, fit layouts tend to work best for a single item that is intended to take up the entire container. This makes them a pretty good layout for child containers, where the parent container controls the overall size and position.

Let's add a bit of complexity to our application and see how this might work.

Adding complexity

For this example, we are going to create a nested container and add it to our card stack. We will also add some buttons to make switching the card stack easier.

Our two new containers are variations on what we already have in our current application. The first is a copy of our hbox layout with a few minor changes:

```
var complexTest =  new Ext.Container({
        layout: {
            type: 'vbox',
```

```
        align: 'stretch'
      },
      style: 'background-color: #FFFFFF',
      items: [{
        xtype: 'container',
        flex: 1,
        html: 'My flex is 1',
        margin: 5,
        style: 'background-color: #7FADCF'
      },
      hboxTest2, {
        xtype: 'container',
        height: 80,
        html: 'My height is 80',
        margin: 5,
        style: 'background-color: #7FADCF'
      }]
    });
```

You can copy and paste our old vboxTest code and change the first line to say complexTest instead of vboxTest. You will also need to remove the second container in our items list (parentheses and all) and replace it with hboxTest2. This is where we will nest another container with its own layout.

Now, we need to define hboxTest2, by copying our previous hboxTest code, and make a few minor changes. You will need to paste this new code up above where you placed the complexTest code, otherwise you will get errors when we try to use hboxTest2, before we actually define it:

```
var hboxTest2 =   new Ext.Container({
        layout: {
            type: 'hbox',
            align: 'stretch'
        },
        flex: 2,
        style: 'background-color: #FFFFFF',
        items: [{
          xtype: 'container',
          flex: 1,
          html: 'My flex is 1',
          margin: 5,
          style: 'background-color: #7FADCF'
        }, {
          xtype: 'container',
          flex: 2,
```

```
                    html: 'My flex is 2',
                    margin: 5,
                    style: 'background-color: #7FADCF'
                }, {
                    xtype: 'container',
                    width: 80,
                    html: 'My width is 80',
                    margin: 5,
                    style: 'background-color: #7FADCF'
                }]
            });
```

After you paste in the code, you will need to change the variable name to hboxTest2, and we will need to add a flex configuration to the main parent container. Since this container is nested within our vbox container, the flex configuration is needed to define how much space hboxTest2 will occupy.

Before we take a look at this new complex layout, let's make our lives a bit easier by adding some buttons to switch between our various layout cards.

Locate layoutPanel and, underneath, where we define the active item, add the following code:

```
dockedItems: [{
            xtype: 'toolbar',
            dock: 'top',
            items: [{
                text: 'hbox',
                handler: function() {
                    var cards = Ext.getCmp('layoutPanel');
                    cards.setActiveItem(0);
                }},{
                text: 'vbox',
                handler: function() {
                    var cards = Ext.getCmp('layoutPanel');
                    cards.setActiveItem(1);
                }
            },{
                text: 'fit',
                handler: function() {
                    var cards = Ext.getCmp('layoutPanel');
                    cards.setActiveItem(2);
                }
            },{
                text: 'complex',
                handler: function() {
```

```
                var cards = Ext.getCmp('layoutPanel');
                cards.setActiveItem(3);
            }
        }],
    }],
```

This code adds a toolbar to the top of our `layoutPanel`, with a button for each of our layout cards.

Each button has a text configuration, which serves as the button's title, and a `handler` configuration. The `handler` configuration defines what happens when the button is clicked. For each of our buttons, we grab the `layoutPanel`, using `Ext.getCmp()`:

```
var cards = Ext.getCmp('layoutPanel');
```

This lets us manipulate our variable `cards`, just as we would manipulate any other panel with a card layout. We can then set the active item in each case by using the following:

```
cards.setActiveItem(x);
```

The `x`, in this case, would be replaced by the index of the item we want to activate (remember that these go in order, starting with zero and not one).

Notice that we also leave the configuration option for `activeItem` in our `layoutPanel` component. This will control which item is displayed when our application starts.

If you refresh the page, you should be able to click through the buttons and see each of our layouts, including the new complex layout.

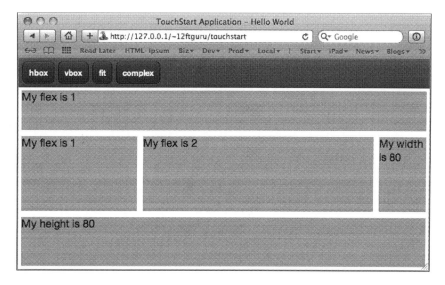

As you can see from this example, our vbox layout splits the window into three rows. The hbox layout, in the second row, splits it into three columns. Using these types of nested layouts makes it pretty easy to create traditional layouts, such as those used in e-mail or social networking applications.

For example, a typical e-mail application can be conceptually broken down into the following:

- An application container with a **Toolbar** and a single container called **Main** with a fit layout.

- The **Main** container will have an hbox layout and two child containers called **Left** and **Right**.

- The **Left** container will have a `flex` of 1 and a vbox layout. It will have two child containers called **Mailboxes** (with a `flex` of 3) and **Activity** (with a `flex` of 1).

- The **Right** container will have a `flex` of 3 and a vbox layout. It will also have two child containers called **Messages** (with a `flex` of 1) and **Message** (with a `flex` of 2).

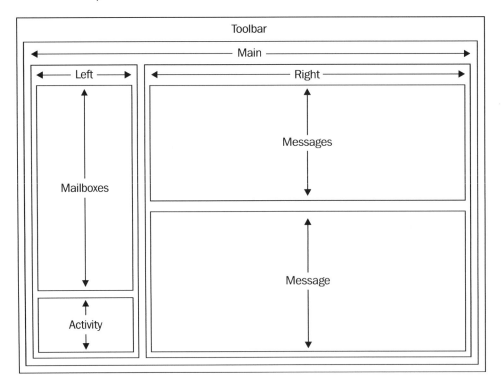

Building container layouts such as these, is good practice. To see example code for this container layout, take a look at the file TouchStart2b.js in the code bundle. It's also a good idea to create some base layouts such as these, to use as templates for getting a jumpstart on building your future applications.

Now that we have a better understanding of layouts, let's take a look at some of the components we can use inside the layouts.

The TabPanel and Carousel components

In our last application, we used buttons and a card layout to create an application that switched between different child items. While it is often desirable for your application to do this programmatically (with your own buttons and code), you can also choose to have Sencha Touch set this up automatically, using TabPanel or Carousel.

TabPanel

TabPanel is useful when you have a number of views the user needs to switch between, such as, contacts, tasks, and settings. The TabPanel component auto-generates the navigation for the layout, which makes it very useful as the main container for an application.

One of our early example applications in *Chapter 2, Creating a Simple Application,* used a simple TabPanel to form the basis of our application. The following is a similar code example:

```
new Ext.Application({
    name: 'TouchStart',
    launch: function() {

        this.viewport = new Ext.TabPanel({
            fullscreen: true,
            cardSwitchAnimation: 'slide',
            tabBar:{
                dock: 'bottom',
                layout: {
                    pack: 'center'
                }
            },
            items: [{
              xtype: 'container',
              title: 'Item 1',
              fullscreen: false,
```

```
                html: 'TouchStart container 1',
                iconCls: 'info'
              }, {
                xtype: 'container',
                html: 'TouchStart container 2',
                iconCls: 'home',
                title: 'Item 2'
              }, {
                xtype: 'container',
                html: 'TouchStart container 3',
                iconCls: 'favorites',
                title: 'Item 3'
              }]
            });
        }
    });
```

TabPanel, in this code, automatically generates a card layout; you don't have to declare a layout. You do need to declare a configuration for the tabBar component. This is where your tabs will automatically appear.

In our previous code example, we dock the toolbar at the bottom. This will generate a large square button for each child item in the items list. The button will also use the iconCls value to assign an icon to the button. The title configuration is used to name the button.

If you dock the tabBar component at the top, it makes the buttons small and round. It also eliminates the icons, even if you declare a value for iconCls, in your child items. Only the title configuration is used when the bar is docked at the top.

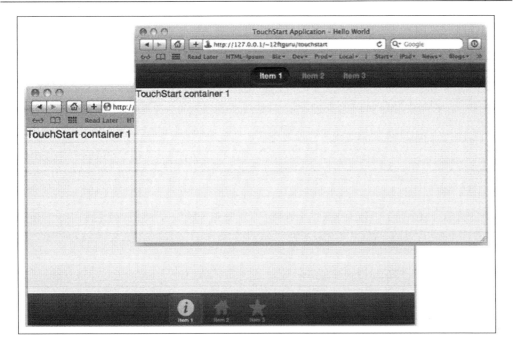

Carousel

The Carousel component is similar to TabPanel, but the navigation it generates is more appropriate for things such as slide shows. It probably would not work as well as a main interface for your application, but it does work well as a way to display multiple items in a single swipeable container.

Similar to TabPanel, Carousel gathers its child items and automatically arranges them in a card layout. In fact, we can actually make just some simple modifications to our previous code to make it into a Carousel:

```
new Ext.Application({
    name: 'TouchStart',
    launch: function() {

        this.viewport = new Ext.Carousel({
            fullscreen: true,
            direction: 'horizontal',
            items: [{
              html: 'TouchStart container 1'
            }, {
```

```
                    html: 'TouchStart container 2'
                }, {
                    html: 'TouchStart container 3'
                }]
            });
        }
    });
```

The first thing we did was create a new `Ext.Carousel` class instead of a new `Ext.TabPanel` class. We also added a configuration for `direction`, which can be either `horizontal` (scrolling from left to right) or `vertical` (scrolling up or down).

We removed the docked toolbar, because, as we will see, `Carousel` doesn't use one. We also removed `iconClass` and `title` from each of our child items for the same reason. Finally, we removed the `xtype` configuration, since the `Carousel` automatically creates a panel for each of its items.

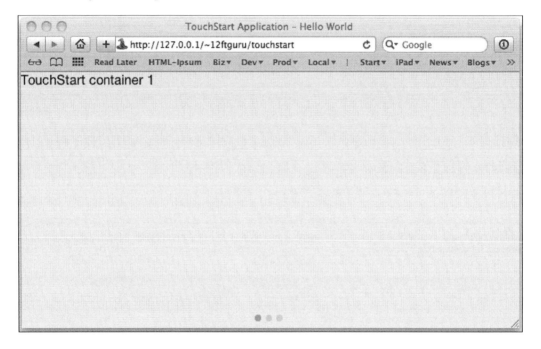

Unlike `TabPanel`, `Carousel` has no buttons, only a series of dots at the bottom, with one dot for each child item. While it is possible to navigate using the dots, the `Carousel` component automatically sets itself up to respond to a swipe on a touch screen. You can duplicate this gesture in the browser by clicking and holding with the mouse, while moving it horizontally. If you declare a `direction: vertical` configuration in your `Carousel`, you can swipe vertically, to move between the child items.

Similar to the card layout in our example at the beginning of the chapter, both the TabPanel and the Carousel components understand the activeItem configuration. This lets you set which item appears when the application first loads. Additionally, they all understand the setActiveItem() method that allows you to change the selected child item after the application loads.

Carousel also has methods for next() and previous(), which allow you to step through the items in order.

It should also be noted that, since TabPanel and Carousel both inherit from the panel, they also understand any methods and configurations that panels and containers understand.

Along with containers and panels, TabPanel and Carousel will serve as the main starting point for most of your applications. However, there is another type of panel you will likely want to use at some point: the FormPanel.

FormPanel

The FormPanel panel is a very specialized version of the panel, and as the name implies, it is designed to handle form elements. Unlike panels and containers, you don't need to specify the layout for FormPanel. It automatically uses its own special form layout.

A basic example of creating a FormPanel would look something like this:

```
var form = new Ext.form.FormPanel({
    items: [
        {
            xtype: 'textfield',
            name : 'first',
            label: 'First name'
        },
        {
            xtype: 'textfield',
            name : 'last',
            label: 'Last name'
        },
        {
            xtype: 'emailfield',
            name : 'email',
            label: 'Email'
        }
    ]
});
```

For this example, we just create the panel and add items for each field in the form. Our xtype tells the form what type of field to create. We can add this to our Carousel and replace our first container, as follows:

```
this.viewport = new Ext.Carousel({
        fullscreen: true,
        direction: 'horizontal',
        items: [form, {
          layout: 'fit',
          html: 'TouchStart container 2'
        }, {
          layout: 'fit',
          html: 'TouchStart container 3'
        }]
    });
```

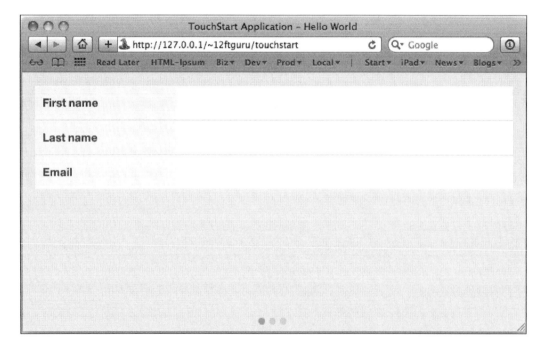

Anyone who has worked with forms in HTML should be familiar with all of the standard field types, so the following xtype attribute names will make sense to anyone who is used to standard HTML forms:

- checkboxfield
- fieldset
- hiddenfield

- passwordfield
- radiofield
- selectfield
- textfield
- textareafield

These field types all match their HTML cousins, for the most part. Sencha Touch also offers a few specialized text fields that can assist with validating the user's input:

- emailfield - Accepts only a valid e-mail address, and on iOS devices, will pull up an alternate e-mail address and URL-friendly keyboard
- numberfield - Accepts only numbers
- urlfield - Accepts only a valid web URL, and also brings up the special keyboard

These special fields will only submit if the input is valid.

All of these basic form fields inherit from the main container class, so they have all of the standard height, width, cls, style, and other container configuration options.

They also have a few field-specific options:

- label - A text label to use with the field
- labelAlign - Where the label appears; this can be top or left, and defaults to left
- labelWidth - How wide the label should be
- name - This corresponds to the HTML name attribute, which is how the value of the field will be submitted
- maxLength - How many characters can be used in the field
- required - If the field is required in order for the form to submit

Form field placement

While FormPanel is typically the container you will use when displaying form elements, you can also place them in any panel or toolbar, if desired. FormPanel has the advantage of understanding the submit() method that will post the form values via AJAX request or POST.

If you include a form field in something that is not a FormPanel, you will need to get and set the values for the field using your own custom JavaScript method.

In addition to the standard HTML fields, there are a few specialty fields available in Sencha Touch. These include the `datepicker`, `slider`, `spinner`, and `toggle` fields.

DatePicker

`datepickerfield` places a clickable field in the form with a small triangle on the far right side.

You can add a date picker to our form by adding the following code after the `emailfield` item:

```
, {
    xtype: 'datepickerfield',
    name : 'date',
    label: 'Date'
}
```

When the user clicks the field, a DatePicker will appear, allowing the user to select a date by rotating the month, day, and year wheels, by swiping up or down.

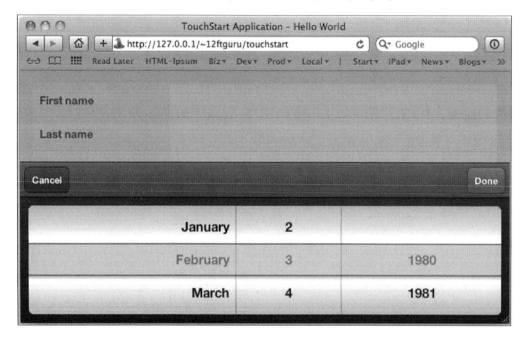

Sliders, spinners, and toggles

Sliders allow for the selection of a single value from a specified numerical range. The `sliderfield` value displays a bar, with an indicator, that can be slid horizontally to select a value. This can be useful for setting volume, color values, and other ranged options.

Like the slider, a spinner allows for the selection of a single value from a specified numerical range. The `spinnerfield` value displays a form field with a numerical value with **+** and **-** buttons on either side of the field.

A toggle allows for a simple selection between one and zero (on and off) and displays a toggle-style button on the form.

Add the following new components to the end of our list of items:

```
,{
    xtype    : 'sliderfield',
    label    : 'Volume',
    value    : 5,
    minValue: 0,
    maxValue: 10
},
{
    xtype: 'togglefield',
    name : 'turbo',
    label: 'Turbo'
},
{
xtype: 'spinnerfield',
minValue: 0,
maxValue: 100,
incrementValue: 2,
cycle: true
}
```

The following screenshot shows how the new components will look:

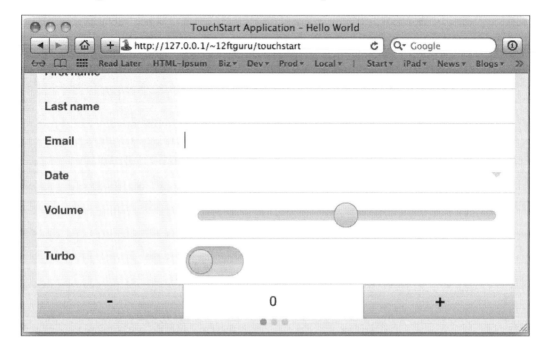

Our `sliderfield` and `spinnerfield` have configuration options for `minValue` and `maxValue`. We also added an `incrementValue` attribute, to `spinnerfield`, that will cause it to move in increments of 2 whenever the + or - button is pressed.

 Using the form fields — We will cover sending and receiving data with forms, later on in the chapters covering data management.

MessageBox and Sheet

At some point, your application will probably need to give feedback to the user, ask the user a question, or alert the user to an event. This is where the `MessageBox` and `Sheet` components come into play.

MessageBox

The `MessageBox` component creates a window, on the page, that can be used to display alerts, gather information, or present options to the user. `MessageBox` can be called in three different ways:

1. `Ext.Msg.alert` takes a title, message text, and an optional callback function to call when the **OK** button on the alert is pressed.

2. `Ext.Msg.prompt` takes a title, message text, and a callback function to call when the **OK** button is pressed. The prompt command creates a text field and adds it to the window automatically. The function, in this case, is passed the text of the field for processing.

3. `Ext.Msg.confirm` takes a title, message text, and a callback function to call when either one of the buttons is pressed.

The callback function

A callback function is a function that gets called automatically, in response to a particular action taken by the user or the code. This is basically the code's way of saying, "When you are finished with this, call me back and tell me what you did". This callback allows the programmer to make additional decisions based on what happened in the function.

Let's try a few examples, starting with a simple message box:

```
new Ext.Application({
    name: 'TouchStart',
    launch: function() {

        this.viewport = new Ext.Panel({
            fullscreen: true,
            dockedItems: [{
            dock: 'top',
            xtype: 'toolbar',
            ui: 'light',
            items: [
                {
                    text: 'Panic',
                    handler: function() {
                        Ext.Msg.alert('Don\'t Panic!', 'Keep Calm. Carry
On.');
                    }
                }
            ]
            }]
        });
    }
});
```

This code sets up a simple panel with a toolbar and a single button. The button has a handler that uses `Ext.Msg.alert()` to show our message box.

Escaping quotes

In our previous example, we use the string `'Don\'t Panic'` as the title for our message box. The `\` tells JavaScript that our second single quote is part of the string and not the end of the string. You can see in the example that the `\` disappears in our message box.

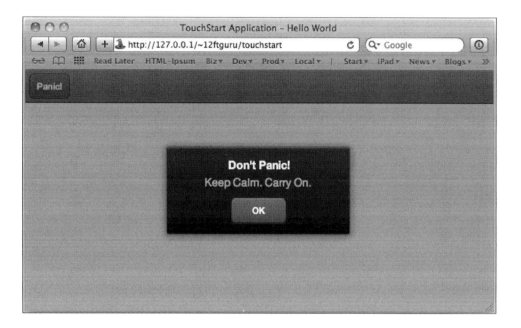

Now, let's add a second button to our `dockedItems` attribute for a `Ext.Msg.prompt` style message box:

```
{
    text: 'Greetings',
    handler: function() {
        Ext.Msg.prompt('Greetings!', 'What is your name?', function(btn,
text) {
            var response = new Ext.MessageBox().show({
            title: 'Howdy',
            msg: 'Pleased to meet you '+text
            });
        });
    }
}
```

This message box is a bit more complex. We create our `Ext.Msg.prompt` class with a title, a message, and a function. The prompt will create our text field automatically, but we need to use the function to determine what to do with the text the user types in the field.

The function is passed a value for the button and a value for the text. Our function grabs the text and creates a new message box to respond, with the name the user typed into the field.

Why is the second MessageBox called differently?

When we call `Ext.Msg`, Sencha Touch creates a temporary object with our title, message, and button. If we attempt to call `Ext.Msg` again, within our response function, Sencha Touch just modifies the existing `promptMessageBox` function. Since we just told that `MessageBox` function to close, our prompt just disappears instead of showing us the new message.

By using `new Ext.MessageBox().show()`, we tell the system we need to create something separate from the original `MessageBox`.

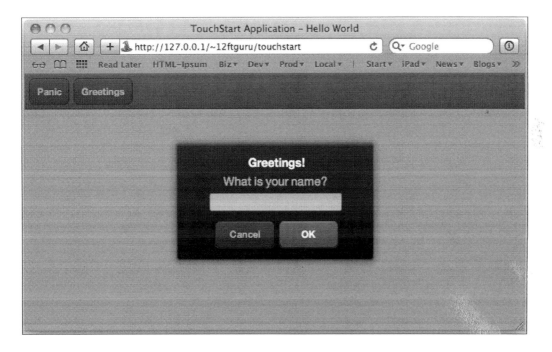

The `Ext.Msg.confirm` MessageBox class is used for decisions the user needs to make or confirmation of a particular action the system is going to take.

Let's add the following component to our list of items in the `dockedItems` component:

```
{
    text: 'Decide',
    handler: function() {
        Ext.Msg.confirm('It\'s Your Choice...', 'Would you like to
proceed?', function(btn) {
            var response = new Ext.MessageBox().show({
                title: 'So be it!',
                msg: 'You chose '+btn
            });
        });
    }
}
```

Similar to the prompt version of the `MessageBox` function, the confirm version takes a title, message, and a callback function. The callback function is passed the button the user pressed (as the value `btn`), which can then be used to determine what steps the system should take next.

In this case, we just toss up a dialog box to display the choice the user has made. You can also use an `if..then` statement to take different actions, depending on which button is pressed.

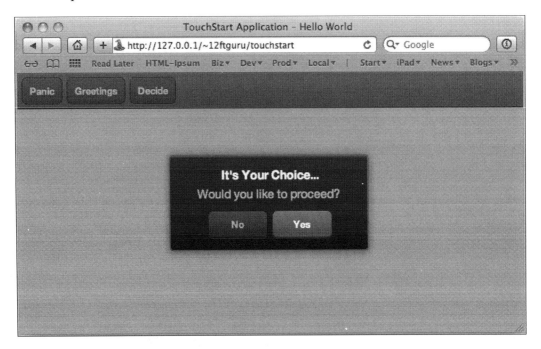

Sheet

The Sheet component is similar to MessageBox function, in that it is typically used to pop up new information or options on the screen. It also presents this new information by appearing over the top of the existing screen. As with MessageBox, no further actions can be taken until Sheet is closed or responded to in some fashion.

Let's add another button to our list of items in the dockedItems component. This button will pop up a new Sheet:

```
{
  text: 'Sheet',
  handler: function() {
    var mySheet = new Ext.Sheet({
      height: 250,
      layout: 'vbox',
      stretchX: true,
      enter: 'top',
      exit: 'top',
      items: [{
        xtype: 'container',
        layout: 'fit',
        flex: 1,
        padding: 10,
        style: 'color: #FFFFFF',
        html: 'A sheet is also a panel. It can do anything the panel
does.'
      }, {
        xtype: 'button',
        height: 20,
        text: 'Close Me',
        handler: function() {
          this.up('sheet').hide();
        }
      }],
      listeners: {
        hide: {
          fn: function(){ this.destroy(); }
        }
      }
    });
    mySheet.show();
  }
}
```

There are a lot of new things here, but some should seem familiar. Our button starts with the text for the button display and then creates a handler that tells the button what to do when clicked.

We then create a new `Ext.Sheet` class. Since `Sheet` inherits from the panel, we have familiar configuration options, such as `height` and `layout`, but we also have a few new options. The `stretchX` and `stretchY` configurations will cause the `Sheet` to expand to the full width (`stretchX`) or height (`stretchY`) of the screen.

The values for `enter` and `exit` control how the `Sheet` component will slide into place on the screen. You can use `top`, `bottom`, `left`, and `right`.

Our `Sheet` uses a vbox layout with two items, a `container` object for our text and a `button` object to hide the `Sheet` component when the user is finished reading it. `button` itself contains an interesting bit of code:

```
this.up('sheet').hide();
```

When we refer to `this`, we are referring to the `button` object, since the function occurs inside the `button` itself. However, we really need to get to the `Sheet` that the button is contained by, in order to close it when the button is clicked. In order to do this, we use a clever little method called `up`.

The `up` method will basically crawl upwards through the structure of the code, looking for the requested item. In this case, we are searching by `xtype` and we have requested the first `Sheet` encountered by the search. We can then hide the `Sheet` with the `hide()` method.

Ext.ComponentQuery

When you want to get one component, and you've given it an ID, you can use `Ext.getCmp()`, as we discussed earlier. If, instead, you want to get multiple components, or one component based on where it is in relation to another component, you can use `query()`, `up()`, and `down()`. To hide a toolbar that's inside a panel you can do the following:

```
panel.down('toolbar').hide();
```

Additionally, to get all toolbars in your application, you could do the following:

```
var toolbars = Ext.ComponentQuery.query('toolbar');
```

Once we hide the Sheet component, we still have a bit of a problem. The Sheet is now hidden, but it still exists in the page. If we go back and click the button again, without destroying the Sheet, we will just keep creating more and more new sheets. That means more and more memory, which also means an eventual death spiral for your application.

What we need to do is make sure we clean up after ourselves, so that the sheets don't pile up. This brings us to the last part of our code and the listeners configuration at the end:

```
listeners: {
        hide: {
            fn: function(){ this.destroy(); }
        }
    }
```

A listener listens for a particular event, in this case, the hide event. When the hide event occurs, the listener then runs the additional code listed in the fn configuration. In this case, we destroy the Sheet using this.destroy();.

We will cover listeners and events in detail, in the next chapter.

A word about this

When we use the variable this in our programs, it always refers to the current item. In the case above, we used this in two separate places, and it referred to two separate objects. In our initial usage, we were inside the configuration options for the button, and so this referred to the button. When we later used this as part of our listener, we were inside the configuration for the sheet, and this referred to the sheet.

If you find yourself getting confused, it can be very helpful to use console.log(this);, to make sure you are addressing the correct component.

You should now be able to click the **Sheet** button and view our new Sheet.

ActionSheet

ActionSheet is a variation on the standard Sheet designed to display a series of buttons. This is a good option when you only need a quick decision from the user, with obvious choices that don't require a lot of explanation. For example, a delete confirmation screen would be a good use for an action sheet.

Let's add a new button to our layout that will pull up an ActionSheet component for a delete confirmation:

```
{
    text: 'ActionSheet',
    handler: function() {
      var actionSheet = new Ext.ActionSheet({
        items: [
            {
                text: 'Delete',
                ui: 'decline'
            },
            {
```

```
                    text: 'Save',
                    ui: 'confirm'
                },
                {
                    text: 'Cancel',
                    handler: function() {
                       this.up('actionsheet').hide();
                    }
                }
            ],
            listeners: {
                hide: {
                    fn: function(){ this.destroy(); }
                }
            }
        });
        actionSheet.show();
        }
    }
```

The `ActionSheet` is created in much the same fashion as our previous `Sheet` example. However, the `ActionSheet` assumes that all of its `items` are buttons, unless you specify a different `xtype`.

Our example has three simple buttons: **Delete**, **Save**, and **Cancel**. The **Cancel** button will hide the `ActionSheet` and the other two buttons are just for show.

As with our previous example, we also want to destroy the `ActionSheet` when we hide it. This prevents copies of the `ActionSheet` from stacking up in the background and creating problems.

Clicking the **ActionSheet** button in our application should now display the
`ActionSheet` we created.

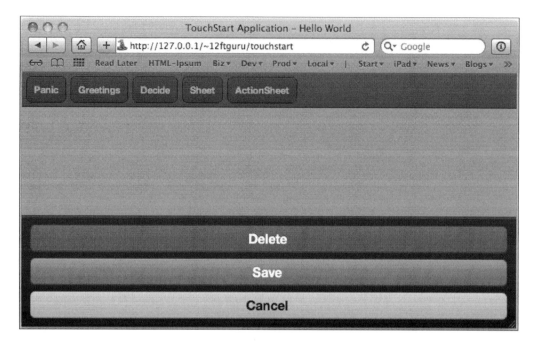

Map

Map is a very specialized container designed to work with the Google Maps API.
The container can be used to display much of the information that Google
Maps displays.

We are going to create a very basic example of the `Map` container for this section,
but we will come back to it in *Chapter 9, Advanced Topics*, and cover some of the
more advanced tricks you can use.

For this example, let's create a new JavaScript file:

```
new Ext.Application({
    name: 'TouchStart',
    launch: function() {
        var map = new Ext.Panel({
        fullscreen: true,
        items    : [
            {
                xtype: 'map',
                useCurrentLocation: true
```

```
            }
        ]});

        this.viewport = map;
    }
});
```

For this example, we are just creating a single `Panel` component with one item. The item is a map and has the configuration `useCurrentLocation: true`. This means that the browser will attempt to use our current location as the center of the map's display. The user is always warned when this happens and given an option to decline.

Before we can see how this works, we need to make one change to our standard `index.html` file. Underneath the line where we include our other JavaScript files, we need to include a new file from Google:

```
<!-- Google Maps API -->
<script type="text/javascript" src="http://maps.google.com/maps/api/
js?sensor=true"></script>
```

This will include all of the functions needed for us to use the Google Maps API.

If you reload the page, you will be asked if you want to allow your current location to be used by the application. Once you accept, you should see a new map with your current location at the center.

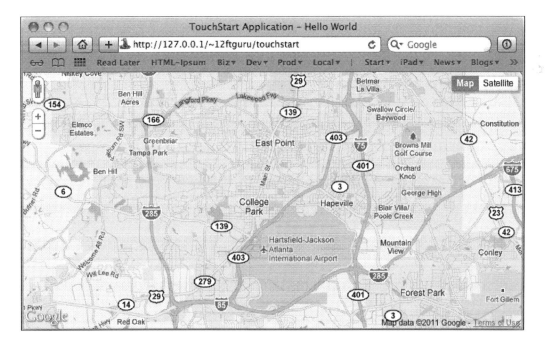

You can also use the map property and the mapOptions configuration option to access the rest of the Google Maps functionality. We will explore some of these options and go into much greater detail in *Chapter 9, Advanced Topics*.

> **Google Maps API documentation**
>
> The full Google Maps API documentation can be found at http://code.google.com/apis/maps/documentation/v3/reference.html.

Lists

Sencha Touch offers a few different kinds of list components. Each of these list components consists of four basic parts: the list panel, an XTemplate, a data store, and a model.

- The list panel is in charge of gathering these other items as part of its configuration options
- The XTemplate determines how each line in the list is displayed
- The data store contains all of the data that will be used in the list
- The model describes the data that gets used in the data store by specifying the datatype (string, Boolean, int, and so on) and any special validation methods or default values

In one of our first examples, we created a list object similar to this one:

```
new Ext.Application({
name: 'TouchStart',
launch: function() {

Ext.regModel('ListItem', {
    fields: [
        {name: 'first', type: 'string'},
        {name: 'last', type: 'string'}
    ]
});

this.viewport = new Ext.Panel({
    fullscreen: true,
    layout: 'fit',
    items: [
    {
```

```
         xtype: 'list',
         itemTpl: '{last}, {first}',
         store: new Ext.data.Store({
           model: 'ListItem',
           data: [
               {first: 'Aaron', last: 'Karp'},
               {first: 'Baron', last: 'Chandler'},
               {first: 'Bryan', last: 'Johnson'},
               {first: 'David', last: 'Evans'},
               {first: 'John', last: 'Clark'},
               {first: 'Norbert', last: 'Taylor'}


           ]
         })
       }]
   });


   }
   });
```

We start by creating our application as before. We then create the model that describes the data we are going to use in our list:

```
Ext.regModel('ListItem', {
    fields: [
        {name: 'first', type: 'string'},
        {name: 'last', type: 'string'}
    ]
});
```

This code gives us three potential values for each ListItem component we will be using in the list: first and last. It also tells us the datatype for each value; in this case, both are strings. This lets the data store know how to handle sorting the data and lets the XTemplate understand how the data can be used.

Once we have our model, we create a panel with a single item, which is our list. The first configuration after our xtype is itemTpl: '{last}, {first}'. This sets our XTemplate for the list to display as: the last name, followed by a comma, and then the first name, for each person in the list. We will cover the XTemplates in greater detail in *Chapter 7, Getting Data Out*.

The `itemTpl` object is followed by our store, which tells the list what data we have available for display. The store also needs a configuration for `model: ListItem;`, so it knows the model we are using. This will allow the store to sort the data correctly.

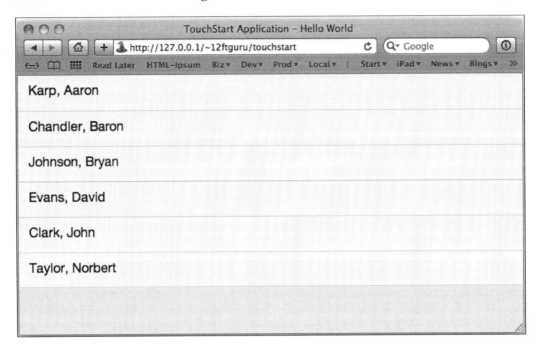

Notice that, right now, our list is not sorted alphabetically. We need to add a sorter to the store underneath the configuration option for our model:

```
sorters: 'last'
```

This will sort our list by the value `last`.

Grouped lists

Grouping lists are also common to a number of applications. Typically, grouping is used for lists of people or other alphabetical lists of items. Address books, or long lists of alphabetical data, are great places for grouped lists. A grouped list places an `indexBar` component on the screen, allowing the user to jump to a specific point in the list.

To group our current list, we need to add two configuration settings to our `list` component. Add the following code beneath where we declare `xtype: 'list'`:

```
grouped: true,
indexBar: true,
```

We also need to add a function to our store that will get the string used to display our alphabetical `indexBar`. Add the following code beneath our `sorters` component in the `store` component:

```
getGroupString : function(record) {
  return record.get('last')[0];
},
```

This code uses `record.get('last')` to get the last name of our contact. We also add `[0]` to the end of our `get` function, which causes JavaScript to treat the last name as an array of individual letters instead of as a string. The first element of our array (`[0]`) is the first letter of the last name for our contact. This lets the list know where to scroll to when one of the letters on the `indexBar` is clicked.

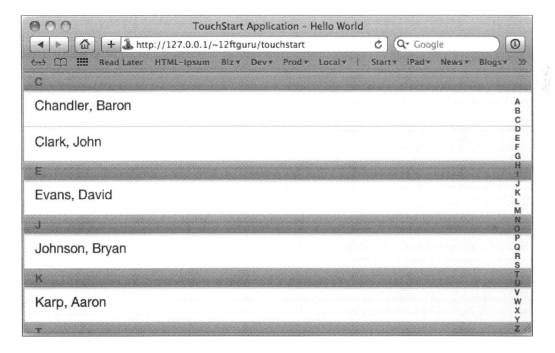

Nested lists

The `NestedList` component automates the layout and navigation of a nested data set. This can be very useful for situations where you have a list of items and details for each item in the list. For example, let's assume we have a list of offices, each office has a set of departments, and each department has people.

We can initially represent this, onscreen, as a list of offices. Clicking on an office takes you to a list of departments within that office. Clicking on a department takes you to a list of people in that department.

The first thing we need is a set of data to use with this list:

```
var data = {
    text: 'Offices',
    items: [{
    text: 'Atlanta Office',
    items: [{
        text: 'Marketing',
        items: [{
            text: 'David Smith',
            leaf: true
            }, {
            text: 'Alex Wallace',
            leaf: true
            }]
        },{
        text: 'Sales',
        items: [{
            text: 'Candice Adams',
            leaf: true
            }, {
            text: 'Mike White',
            leaf: true
            }]
        }
    ]
    },{
    text: 'Athens Office',
    items: [{
        text: 'IT',
        items: [{
            text: 'Baron Chandler',
            leaf: true
            }, {
            text: 'Aaron Karp',
            leaf: true
            }]
        },{
        text: 'Executive',
        items: [{
```

```
            text: 'Bryan Johnson',
            leaf: true
            }, {
            text: 'John Clark',
            leaf: true
            }]
        }
    ]
  }]
};
```

This is a rather large and ugly-looking array of data, but it can be broken down into a few simple pieces:

- We have one main item called `Offices`
- `Offices` has a list of two items, `Atlanta Office` and `Athens Office`
- The two items each have two departments
- Each department has two people

Each of our people in this list has a special attribute called `leaf`. The `leaf` attribute tells our program that it has reached the end of the nested data. Additionally, every item in our list has an attribute called `text`. This becomes important for both our data model and our store.

Since we are only worried about displaying the value of `text`, our model becomes very simple:

```
Ext.regModel('ListItem', {
    fields: [{name: 'text', type: 'string'}]
});
```

We can then create our store and add our data to it:

```
var store = new Ext.data.TreeStore({
    model: 'ListItem',
    root: data,
    proxy: {
        type: 'ajax',
        reader: {
            type: 'tree',
            root: 'items'
        }
    }
});
```

For a `NestedList` we need to use a `TreeStore` and set the `reader` to use `type: 'tree'`. We set the `root` configuration to point to the variable data we defined earlier. We also need to tell the store where it should start looking for data. In this case, we set `root: 'items'` to tell the store proxy to begin looking in the first set of items in our data.

Finally, we need to create our `NestedList`:

```
var nestedList = new Ext.NestedList({
    fullscreen: true,
    title: 'Minions',
    displayField: 'text',
    store: store
});
```

We set the `NestedList` component to fullscreen, we set a title, we tell it what field to display, and finally, we point it to our store so it can grab the data we made.

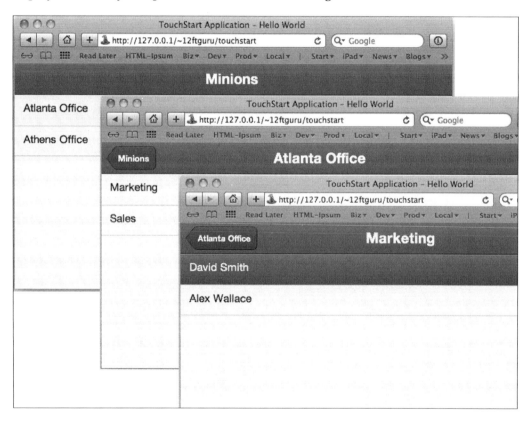

If you click through the nested list, you will notice that the click actions have been added automatically, as well as the upper navigation and titles.

The NestedList provides a great starting point for displaying hierarchical data quickly and efficiently on a small screen.

Finding more information with the Sencha API

We have covered quite a bit of information in this chapter, but it's only a fraction of the information that is available to you in the Sencha Touch API documentation.

At first, the API can seem a bit overwhelming, but if you understand the organization, you can find the information you need, quickly. Here are a couple of tips to get you started.

Finding a component

The left-hand side of the API is where you will browse and search for components.

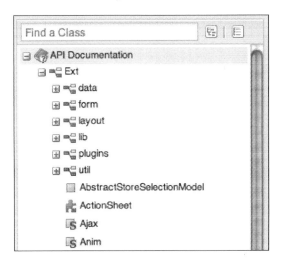

Currently, the API only searches for words that begin with the search term. This can be a bit frustrating since a search for "List" will not bring up the NestedList component. This shortcoming will be addressed in the next major release, but until then, it's important to remember when you are searching.

You can also browse by expanding and collapsing the items in the list. The buttons near the top will expand or collapse all of the items in the list.

Understanding the component page

The information at the top of the individual component page provides a huge jump-start in understanding how the component works.

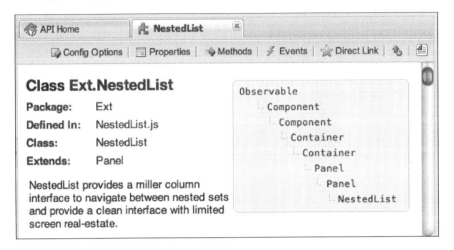

A quick scan of the component hierarchy, on the right, will tell you which other items the component inherits from. If you understand the base components, such as the container and panel, you can quickly use that knowledge to guide you through using the new component.

The buttons at the top of this section will jump automatically to the sections for:

- **Config Options** - The initial options that are used when the component is created
- **Properties** - The information you can gather from the component after it is created
- **Methods** - The things the component knows how to do, once it's created
- **Events** - The things the component pays attention to, once it's created

There is also a direct link button that will let you copy a direct link to the page you are viewing. This can be helpful when sharing information.

Most of the common components also include examples at the top of the page.

Using these bits of information should provide you with a starting point for learning any component in the API.

Summary

In this chapter, we began with a look at the base component called `Ext.Component`. We also showed how to grab a component after it gets created, so we can manipulate it as needed. We then explored the layout for containers in more detail, showing how it affects the child items inside the container.

The chapter also described a number of the more common and useful components in Sencha Touch, including:

- Containers
- Panels
- `TabPanel`
- `Carousel`
- `FormPanel`
- `FormItem`
- `MessageBox`
- `Sheet`
- `List`
- `NestedList`

We closed out the chapter with a bit of advice on using the Sencha Touch API.

In the next chapter, we will cover the use of events in Sencha Touch.

5
Events

In the previous chapter, we took a closer look at the components available in Sencha Touch. However, simply creating components isn't enough to build an application. The components still need to communicate with each other in order to make our application do anything truly useful. This is where events come into play.

In this chapter, we will examine events in Sencha Touch: what they are, why we need them, and how they work. We will discuss how to use listeners and handlers to make your application react to the user's touch as well as to events happening behind the scenes. We will also cover some helpful concepts such as observable capture and event delegation. We will finish up with a walkthrough of the touch-specific events and a look at how you can get more information from the Sencha Touch API.

The chapter will cover the following points:

- Events
- Listeners and handlers
- Ext.util.Observable
- Event delegation
- Touch-specific events
- Additional information on events

What are events?

As programmers, we tend to think of code as an orderly sequence of instructions, executing one line, and then the next, and the next. It's easy to lose sight of the fact that our code really spends a lot of time sitting and waiting for the user to do something. It's waiting for the user to press a button, open a window, or select from a list. The code is waiting for an event.

Typically, an event occurs right before or right after a component performs a specific task. When the task is performed, the event is broadcast to the rest of the system, where it can trigger specific code or be used by other components to trigger new actions.

For example, a button in Sencha Touch will trigger an event whenever it is tapped. This tap can execute code inside the button that creates a new dialog box, or a panel component can "listen" to what the button is doing and change its color when it "hears" the button trigger a `tap` event.

Given that most applications are intended for human interaction, it's safe to say that a lot of the functionality of your programs will come from responding to events. From a user's perspective, the events are what make the program actually "do" something. The program is responding to the user's request.

In addition to responding to requests, events also have an important role to play in making sure that things happen in the correct order.

Asynchronous versus synchronous

Albert Einstein once remarked, "The only reason for time is so that everything doesn't happen at once". While this might seem like an offhand comment, it actually has a great deal of relevance when it comes to writing code.

As we write our code in Sencha Touch, we are directing the web browser to create and destroy components on the user's screen. The obvious limitation of this process is that we cannot manipulate a component before it gets created, nor after it's destroyed.

This seems pretty straightforward at first glance. You would never write a line of code that tries to talk to a component on the line *before* you actually create the component, so what's the problem?

The problem has to do with asynchronous actions within the code. While most of our code will execute sequentially or in a synchronous fashion, there are a number of cases where we will need to send out a request and get back a response before we can proceed. This is especially true in web-based applications.

For example, let's say we have a line of code that builds a map using a request from Google Maps. We will need to wait until we have received a response from Google and rendered our map before we can begin fiddling about with it. However, we don't want the rest of our application to freeze while we wait on the response. So, we make an asynchronous request, one that happens in the background, while the rest of our application goes about its business.

These asynchronous requests are called AJAX requests. **AJAX** stands for **Asynchronous JavaScript and XML**. If we configure one of our buttons to send out an AJAX request, the user can still do other things while the application is waiting for a response.

On the interface side of things, you will probably want to let the user know that we made the request and are currently waiting for a response. In most cases, this means displaying a "loading" message or animated graphic.

Using events in Sencha Touch, we can show the loading graphic by tying into the `beforerequest` event in the AJAX component. Since we need to know when to make the loading message disappear, our component will wait for the `requestcomplete` event from our AJAX request. Once that event fires, we can execute some code to tell the loading message to go away. We can also use the `requestexception` event to inform the user whether errors occurred during the request.

Using this type of event-driven design allows you to respond quickly to the user's actions, without making them wait for some of the more time-consuming requests your code needs to perform. You can also use the events to inform the user of errors. The key to events is getting your other components to "listen" for the event, and then telling them how to handle the information they receive.

Listeners and handlers

Every component in Sencha Touch has a long list of events that it generates. Given the number of components you will likely have in your application, a lot of chatter is going on.

Imagine a party with 100 people, all having lots of different conversations. Now imagine trying to pick out all of the useful information from each conversation. It's impossible. You have to focus on a specific conversation in order to gather anything useful.

In much the same way, components also have to be told what to listen for, or else, such as our unfortunate partygoer, they would quickly be overwhelmed. Fortunately for us, there's a confguration for that.

A `listeners` configuration tells the component what events it needs to pay attention to. Listeners can be added like any other configuration option in Sencha Touch. For example, the configuration option on a panel might look like the following:

```
listeners: {
  tap: {
element: 'body',
```

```
fn: function(){ Ext.Msg.alert('Single Tap'); }
  }
}
```

This configuration option tells the panel to listen for the `tap` event, when the user taps once on the `body` element of the panel. When the `tap` event occurs, we execute the function listed in the `fn` configuration option (this is typically referred to as a handler). In this case, we pop up a message box with the words **Single Tap**.

Notice that the items in our `listeners` configuration are always part of an object (curly braces on either side), even if there is only one event we are listening for. If we were to add a second event, it would look like the following:

```
listeners: {
  tap: {
   element: 'body',
   fn: function(){ Ext.Msg.alert('Single Tap'); }
  },
  hide: {
   fn: function(){ this.destroy(); }
  }
}
```

We can also get information back from the listener and use it in our handler functions. For example, the `tap` event sends back the `event` object, the DOM element that was clicked, and the `listener` object itself, if we have the following listener on a panel:

```
listeners: {
   tap: {
     element: 'body',
     fn: function(event, div, listener) {
       console.log(event, div, listener);
     }
   }
}
```

When the user taps inside the panel, we will get the following information on the console:

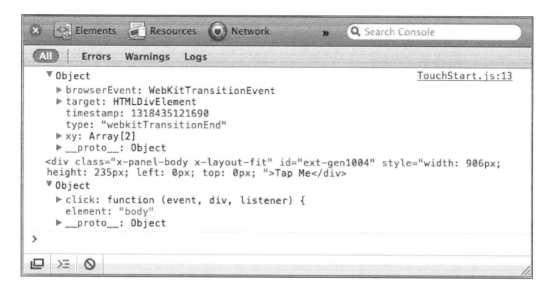

Arguments for events

You will notice that certain values are passed to our event by default. These default values can be found in the Sencha Touch API event documentation for each component, at http://docs.sencha.com/touch/1-1/.

Each event will have its own default values. Select a component from the Sencha API documentation, and then click **Events** at the top of the page, to see a list of all events for the component. The description of each event will include its default arguments.

As you can see from the console, our `event` object contains a Unix timestamp for when the tap occurred, the `x` and `y` coordinates of the tap itself, as well as the entire content of the `div` tag that was tapped. You may have also noticed that our `tap` event is referred to as a `click` event in our debug output. In Sencha Touch, the `tap` and `click` events are aliased to one another. This preserves compatibility between the desktop browser's traditional `click` event and the mobile browser's `tap` event.

We can use all of this information inside our function.

For this example, we will create a simple panel with a red container. Our tap listener will change the size of the red box to match where we tap on the screen:

```
new Ext.Application({
  name: 'TouchStart',
  launch: function() {
    var eventPanel = new Ext.Panel({
      fullscreen: true,
      layout: 'auto',
      items: [{
        xtype: 'container',
        width: 40,
        height: 40,
        id: 'tapTarget',
        style: 'background-color: #800000;',
      }],
      id: 'eventPanel',
      listeners: {
tap: {
        element: 'body',
        fn: function(event, div, listener) {
            var cmp = Ext.getCmp('tapTarget');
            cmp.setWidth(event.xy[0]);
            cmp.setHeight(event.xy[1]);
            console.log(event.xy);
        }
      }
     }
    });
    this.viewport = eventPanel;
  }
});
```

If we run this code with the console open, we can see that the X and Y coordinates of where we tap appear in the console. Our box also grows or shrinks to match these values.

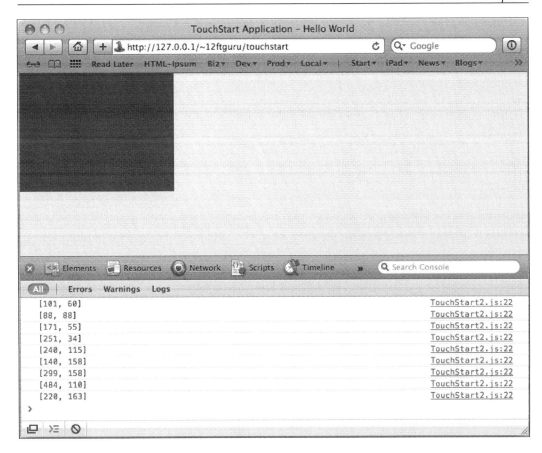

As you can see from the code, we listen for the `tap` event. We then grab the
`container` component using `Ext.getCmp('tapTarget');`, and change the size,
based on the value we got back from the `tap` event:

```
tap: {
  element: 'body',
  fn: function(event, div, listener) {
   var cmp = Ext.getCmp('tapTarget');
   cmp.setWidth(event.xy[0]);
   cmp.setHeight(event.xy[1]);
   console.log(event.xy);
  }
}
```

Since `event.xy` is an array, we need to grab the individual values using
`event.xy[0]` and `event.xy[1]`.

Adding listeners and events dynamically

Listeners can also be added to a component dynamically. If we were to add a new listener to our previous example, it would look something as the following:

```
var cmp = Ext.getCmp('tapTarget');
cmp.on('resize',
function() {
var h = this.getHeight();
var w = this.getWidth();
this.update('height: '+h+'<br>width: '+w)
}, cmp);
```

This code will get the height and width of the container. It will then use the `update` method to add the height and width as text to the container, when the `resize` event fires.

However, there is one slight problem with this approach: the `resize` event only fires when a container is manually resized by dragging the lower-left corner of a manually-resizable container. Since ours is changed programmatically, the `resize` event is never fired.

We can fix this by manually firing the event in our previous code using the `fireEvent()` method:

```
listeners: {
  tap: {
    element: 'body',
    fn: function(event, div, listener) {
      var cmp = Ext.getCmp('tapTarget');
      cmp.setWidth(event.xy[0]);
      cmp.setHeight(event.xy[1]);
      console.log(event.xy);
      cmp.fireEvent('resize');
    }
  }
}
```

The `fireEvent()` method can be used with both existing events as well as your own custom events.

Custom events

While Sencha Touch components respond to a large number of events, it can sometimes be helpful to fire custom events within your application.

For example, you could fire a custom event called `vikinginvasion`, using the same type of syntax as our previous example:

```
cmp.fireEvent('vikinginvasion');
```

You can then add a listener in your code for `vikinginvasion`, along with a function to handle the event:

```
var cmp = Ext.getCmp('tapTarget');
 cmp.on('vikinginvasion',
 function() {
alert("Man The gates!");
 }, this);
```

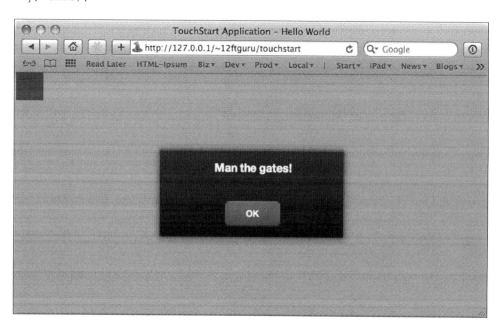

You can also check a component to see if it has a specific listener, using the `hasListener()` method:

```
var cmp = Ext.getCmp('tapTarget');
if(cmp.hasListener('vikinginvasion') {
  console.log('Component is alert for invasion');
} else {
  console.log('Component is asleep at its post');
}
```

There are also a number of helpful options you can use to control how the listeners will check for events.

Listener options

For the most part, listeners can simply be configured with the event name, handler, and scope, but sometimes you need a bit more control. Sencha Touch provides a number of helpful options to modify how the listener works:

- `delay`: This will delay the handler from acting after the event is fired. It is given in milliseconds.

- `single`: This provides a one-shot handler that executes after the next event fires and then removes itself.

- `buffer`: This causes the handler to be scheduled to run as part of an `Ext.util.DelayedTask` component. This means that if an event is fired, we wait a certain amount of time before we execute the handler. If the same event fires again within our delay time, we reset the timer before executing the handler (only once).

- `element`: This allows us to specify a specific element within the component. For example, we can specify a body within a panel for a `tap` event. This would ignore taps to the docked items and only listen for a tap on the body of the panel.

- `target`: This will limit the listener to the events coming from the target and it will ignore the same event coming from any of its children.

Using the different listener options would look something like the following:

```
var cmp = Ext.getCmp('tapTarget');
cmp.on('vikinginvasion', this.handleInvasion, this, {
single: true,
delay: 100
});
```

This example would add a listener for `vikinginvasion` and execute a function called `this.handleInvasion`. The handler would only execute once, after a 100-millisecond delay. It would then remove itself from the component.

This basic list of configuration options gives you quite a bit of flexibility when adding listeners. However, there is one additional configuration option available in listeners that will require a bit more explanation. It's called `scope`.

Scope

Within your handler function is a special variable called `this`. Usually, `this` refers to the component that fired the event, in which case, the `scope` would typically be set to `scope: this`. However, it's possible to specify a different value for `scope` in your listener configuration. From our previous example, a change in `scope` might look like the following:

```
tap: {
 element: 'body',
 scope: eventPanel,
 fn: function(event, div, listener) {
  this.setWidth(event.xy[0]);
  this.setHeight(event.xy[1]);
  console.log(event.xy);
 }
}
```

In this example, the `scope` (and as such, the variable `this`) has been changed to our `eventPanel` component. We can now set values directly, instead of having to use `Ext.getCmp('tapTarget');` to get the panel at the beginning of our function.

We can also set the `scope` component in a similar fashion, by using the `on` method to add a listener:

```
var myPanel = new Ext.Panel({...});
var button = new Ext.Button({...});

button.on('click', function() {
   console.log('This should be myPanel:', this);
}, myPanel);
```

Here, we added `myPanel` as an argument after the handler definition, which means that when the `click` event is fired and the handler function is called, you will be able to access `myPanel` by referring to `this`.

Within handler functions, you aren't guaranteed to have access to the same variables when you define the function. Changing the scope of a function can allow you to access a specific variable that's not easy to get to with `Ext.getCmp()` or `Ext.get()`. It can also be a simple convenience for getting to the component you are most likely to use in the function.

While `scope` may be a hard concept to grasp, it is a very useful part of the listener configurations.

Removing listeners

Normally, listeners are removed automatically when a component is destroyed. However, sometimes you will want to remove the listener before the component is destroyed. To do so, you'll need a reference to the handler function you created the listener with.

So far, we've been using anonymous functions to create our listeners, but if we're going to remove the listener, we have to do it a bit differently:

```
var myPanel = new Ext.Panel({…});

var myHandler = function() {
  console.log('myHandler called.');
};

myPanel.on('click', myHandler);
```

This can be a good practice, since it allows you to define the handler functions once and reuse them wherever you need them. It also allows you to remove the handler later:

```
myPanel.removeListener('click', myHandler);
```

 In Sencha parlance, `on()` is an alias for `addListener()` and `un()` is an alias for `removeListener()`, meaning that they do the exact same thing. Feel free to use whichever you prefer, when dealing with events.

Managed listeners

In some cases, listeners are part of a relationship between two objects, and when one of the objects is destroyed, the listener is no longer necessary.

For example, say you have two panels, `panel1` and `panel2`, and you want to change the size of `panel1` to match the size of `panel2`, whenever `panel2` is resized. You could put a listener on the `resize` event for `panel2`, but if `panel1` were to be destroyed, the listener would still be there.

You could add an additional listener to `panel1` that would wait for the `destroy` event and then remove the listener from `panel2`, but that could become cumbersome quickly.

You can get around this particular problem by using a managed listener. A managed listener works a little bit differently from a regular listener:

```
var panel1 = new Ext.Panel({…});
var panel2 = new Ext.Panel({…});

panel1.addManagedListener(panel2, 'resize',
  function() {
  console.log('Panel 2 was resized.');
panel1.setSize(panel2.getSize());
  }
);
```

This can get a bit confusing, because when we call `panel1.on()` or `panel1.addListener()`, we're adding a listener to `panel1`. However, when we call `addManagedListener()`, the first argument is actually a different component we're adding the listener to. In this case, we're adding a `resize` listener to `panel2` that will automatically be removed if `panel1` is destroyed.

Essentially, `addManagedListener` adds listeners that clean up after themselves, which can help greatly with memory management.

Handlers and buttons

As you might have noticed from some of our previous code, buttons have a default configuration called `handler`. This is because the purpose of a button is generally to be clicked or tapped. The `handler` configuration is just useful shorthand for adding the `tap` listener. As such, the following two pieces of code do exactly the same thing:

```
var button = new Ext.button({
text: 'press me',
  handler: function() {
    this.setText('Pressed');
  }
})

var button = new Ext.button({
  text: 'press me',
  listener: {
tap: {
      fn: function() {
        this.setText('Pressed');
      }
    }
  }
});
```

This same default handler behavior applies to tabs as well. The handler simply serves as a quick way to access the most routinely used event for the component.

Suspending and queuing events

Sometimes, you will want to keep components from firing events. Perhaps you want to do some additional processing on data returned from an AJAX query, or you want to write some custom code to handle resizing your component. `Observable` gives you a way to do so via the `suspendEvents()` and `resumeEvents()` methods. You can call these methods on any object that extends `Observable`, such as a panel:

```
var myPanel = new Ext.Panel({...});

myPanel.suspendEvents();

myPanel.setHeight(100);
myPanel.setWidth(100);

myPanel.resumeEvents();
```

Normally, the `setHeight()` and `setWidth()` functions cause the `resize` event to fire. In this example, though, we essentially put the panel to sleep while we resize it, and then wake it back up when we're done. In this case, the `resize` event will never fire, so any components listening for that event will never hear it.

Note that we only suspended events on the `myPanel` object. If we had resized another panel at the same time, then that panel's events would still have fired.

This is very useful when you need to do things behind the scenes in your application, but sometimes you'll want to have the events fire after you're done with your work, so that the other components can catch up. In that case, simply pass `true` as the argument to `suspendEvents()`:

```
myPanel.on('resize', function() {
  console.log('Resized!');
});

myPanel.suspendEvents(true);

myPanel.setHeight(100);
myPanel.setHeight(100);
console.log('Resuming Events.');
myPanel.resumeEvents();
```

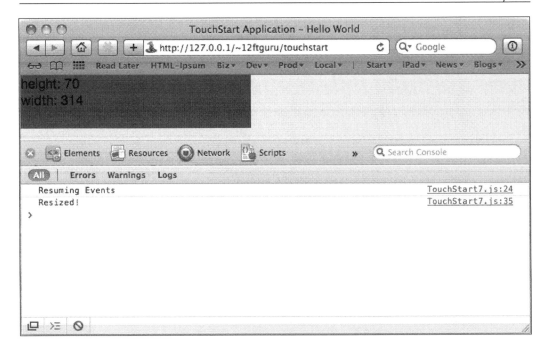

You can see how the **Resuming Events** line comes before the resize events. This is because we didn't fire any events until after the console.log() and resumeEvents() calls.

You should be very careful with suspending events. Much of the built-in Sencha Touch functionality relies heavily on events, and suspending them can cause unexpected behavior.

Common events

Let's take a look at our old friend Ext.Component and see some of the common events available to us. Remember, since most of our components will inherit from Ext.Component, these events will be common across most of the components we use.

Most of our events will fall into two categories. The first set of events revolves around the creation of the component.

When the web browser executes your Sencha Touch code, it writes the components into the web page as a series of div, span, and other standard HTML tags. These elements are also linked to code within Sencha Touch that standardizes the look and functionality of the component for all supported web browsers. This process is referred to as rendering the component.

This rendering takes place in a number of stages, each of which fires an event:

- `beforerender`: Before the render process begins
- `added`: When the component is added to the container
- `beforeactivate`: Before the component is visually activated
- `activate`: When the component is visually activated
- `render`: After the component's HTML is rendered
- `afterrender`: After rendering is finished

These events give you a number of places to interact with your component before, during, and after the rendering process.

The second set of events is concerned with the actions taken by or done to the component itself. These events include:

- `show`: Fires when the `show` method is used on the component
- `hide`: Fires when the `hide` method is used on the component
- `destroy`: Fires when the component is destroyed
- `disable`: Fires when the `disable` method is used on the component
- `enable`: Fires when the `enable` method is used on the component
- `orientationchange`: Fires when the orientation of the device is changed
- `remove`: Fires when the component is removed from a container
- `resize`: Fires after the component is resized

These events provide a way to base the actions of your code on what is being done by, or done to, your components.

Each component will also have some specific events associated with it. For a list of these events, please consult the API docs at `http://docs.sencha.com/touch/1-1/`. Just select a component from the list on the left side and click the **Events** button at the top of the page.

Ext.util.Observable

`Ext.util.Observable` is the base class that handles listening to, and firing of, events for all Sencha Touch components. Any class that fires events extends `Ext.util.Observable`. For the most part, you won't need to directly use `Ext.util.Observable` itself, since it comes built into almost every Sencha Touch component, but there are a few cases where using it directly can make things easier.

Centralizing event handling with Observe

Sometimes, over the course of building an application, you will find yourself adding the same listeners to the same kind of objects multiple times. For large applications, this can take up quite a bit of memory. That's where `Ext.util.Observable.observe()` comes in. This method will allow you to add listeners to a class, instead of a particular instance of that class. Normally, when we add listeners, we do something such as this:

```
var panel = new Ext.Panel({...});
panel.on('resize', function(){...});
```

The listener will only run if that exact panel is resized. To add a listener to all `Ext.Panel` components, you can pass the component constructor you want to observe, then add your listeners:

```
Ext.util.Observable.observe(Ext.Panel);
Ext.Panel.on('resize', function(){...});
```

You'll notice that we didn't create a new panel here. Instead, we added the `resize` listener to `Ext.Panel` itself. Now, any panel you create with the new `Ext.Panel()` component, it will have the `resize` listener enabled automatically.

Additionally, this gives you a single place to update when you need to make changes to the `resize` listener and function. This type of class-based listener can save time, memory, and a lot of headaches.

Capture: a tool for debugging

`Ext.util.Observable.capture` is a static method. This means you won't have to create a new instance of an object—you can call it directly. This method will call a handler for every single event that an object fires, which can come in handy when you're trying to figure out if you've added listeners to the proper event and if those events are firing.

Using our resizing `eventPanel` example, add the following line after `this.viewport` = `eventPanel;`:

```
Ext.util.Observable.capture(eventPanel, function() {
  console.log('The eventPanel fired an Event:', arguments);
});
```

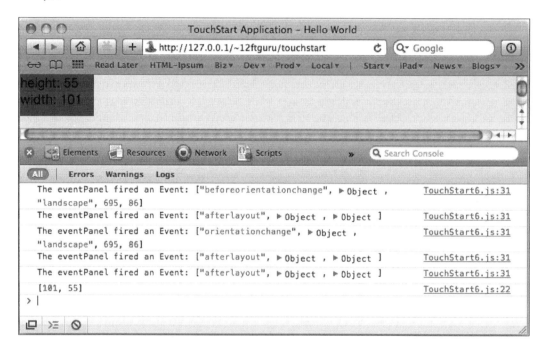

As you can see, this generates a lot of console lines. The first argument to the function will always be the event name, and the subsequent arguments will be the arguments that are typically passed to that particular event. If you want to start capturing events only after a certain known event fires, you can add the `capture` statement to a listener. For example, if you wanted to only start capturing events after the panel was rendered, you would do something such as the following:

```
listeners: {
  render: {
    fn: function(myPanel) {
      Ext.util.Observable.capture(eventPanel,
      function() {
        console.log('The eventPanel fired an Event:', arguments);
      });
    }
  }
}
```

Now, `Ext.util.Observable.capture` will only be started once the `render` event has fired. From that point on, it will continue to capture all events fired by the panel.

You can stop capturing with `Ext.util.Observable.releaseCapture()`, as well. Say we want to stop capturing events after a `resize` event. Then, in our `capture` function, we could do the following:

```
Ext.util.Observable.capture(eventPanel, function() {
  console.log('The eventPanel fired an Event:', arguments);
    if (arguments[0] == 'resize') {
      Ext.util.Observable.releaseCapture(eventPanel);
    }
});
```

 Even with `releaseCapture()` handy, you want to be very sure to remove any `capture` statements from your code before deploying in production, as they can be very memory- and processor-intensive.

Event delegation

When a component in Sencha Touch fires an event, the event "bubbles up" the chain to the parent component. This gives us some interesting opportunities with regards to memory and efficiency.

Events and memory

One of the common uses of event delegation is in lists. Let's say, we have a list of people such as those you would find in a common address book. When a name in the address book is clicked, we switch to the details panel with all of the contact information. This is a pretty straightforward setup most of us would recognize.

However, let's say we want to add a phone icon to each of our list items. When the phone icon gets clicked, the person's phone number is dialed. You might be inclined to add a `click` handler for each icon, but this is a very bad idea, because all of those listeners take up space in memory.

An address book with 400 people would have 400 listeners. This will slow down a web-based application, as it tries to listen to 400 separate elements within the DOM (in addition to everything else in your code that has a listener).

However, you can get around this problem using event delegation.

Delegating events

Let's start with a very simplified version for our contact list:

```
var contactList = new Ext.List({
  tpl: '<tpl for="."><li><img src="images/phone.
png"/><h1>{contactName}</h1></li></tpl>',
  listeners: {
    el: {
      tap: callContact,
      delegate: 'img'
    }
  }
});
```

Unlike our previous examples, where we instructed the component which event to listen to, in this case, we tell the component where to listen for the event. In this case, we chose el, which is a property common to all components and basically means within the item (we could also use body).

Now that the component knows where to listen, we tell it what to listen for on the line tap: callContact. This also tells the List component what to run when the tap event occurs.

The last line, delegate: 'img' delegates the event to any img tag inside our List component. In this case, it would be our phone.png icon on each row of the list.

The result is a single listener, which checks to see if an image is tapped in our list.

This saves on memory, and also means that if you add or remove any list items, you don't have to add and remove listeners, too.

Touch-specific events

In addition to component events, Sencha Touch also understands a number of touch-specific events. These events include:

- touchstart: An event that records the initial contact point with the device.
- touchend: An event that records where the contact ended on the device.
- touchmove: An event that records where the touch moved (this one will fire off as a series of events that map the path of the user's touch along the screen).
- touchdown: An event that records when the element is touched as part of a drag or swipe.

- `dragstart`: An event that records when the element is initially dragged.
- `drag`: Similar to `touchmove`, `drag` tracks the path of the element, when dragged.
- `dragend`: An event that records where the element stopped being dragged.
- `singletap`: A single tap on the screen. This will fire once for the first tap, when a screen is double-tapped. It will not fire on the second tap.
- `tap`: A tap on the screen. This will fire both for the first and second tap, when a screen is double tapped.
- `doubletap`: Two quick taps on the screen.
- `taphold`: A tap and hold on the screen.
- `tapcancel`: An event that fires when you stop tap holding.
- `swipe`: A single finger brushed across the screen from left to right.
- `pinch`: Two fingers brought together in a pinching motion.
- `pinchstart`: Where the pinch started.
- `pinchend`: Where the pinch ended.

There is one small caveat to note with these touch-specific events: with the exception of `tap` and `doubletap`, Sencha Touch is actually receiving the events from the web browser rather than the component itself. Since the web browser is doing our listening for us, we need to attach our listener to something the web browser understands.

This means that instead of binding the event to the component itself, we have to bind the event to the underlying element of the component.

Component versus element

One of the harder concepts for people new to web programming is the relationship between the web browser and the Sencha Touch components. At its core, when a Sencha Touch component is rendered in the web browser, it gets translated into a complex series of `div` and `span` that the web browser can read and display. When we refer to the underlying element of the component, we are talking about one of these `div` containers.

Since a WebKit-based browser, such as Safari or Chrome, is designed to understand all of our touch-specific events, the Sencha Touch component can be instructed to monitor a `div` tag on the web page to see if these events occur.

Additionally, since the component can only monitor a `div` tag, it can only do it after the `div` tag has been rendered to the web page. This means we have to set our component to listen for the `render` event, and then tell it to add the monitoring. It looks something like the following:

```
new Ext.Application({
  name: 'TouchStart',
  launch: function() {
    var eventPanel = new Ext.Panel({
      fullscreen: true,
      layout: 'fit',
      html: 'Tap Me',
      id: 'eventPanel',
      listeners: {
        afterRender: function() {
          this.mon(this.el, {
          swipe: this.event2Console
          });
        }
      },
      event2Console: function(e) {
        console.log(e);
      }
    });
    this.viewport = eventPanel;
  }
});
```

We create our panel, as usual, and we add a listener for `afterRender`. This tells the panel that, once it exists within the browser window, it should execute the following code (in this case, we want it to run):

```
this.mon(this.el, {
  swipe: this.event2Console
});
```

This will cause Sencha Touch to listen for browser events generated by panel's DOM element, rather than the panel itself. The element then listens for the `swipe` event to occur. When the `swipe` event occurs, we execute our function `this.event2Console`.

Notice that we did things a bit differently this time. Usually, we create the function as part of the listener:

```
this.mon(this.el, {
  swipe: function(e) {
    console.log(e);
  }
}
```

Instead of that, we added the function onto the component itself, just as a configuration object:

```
event2Console: function(e) {
  console.log(e);
}
```

We then referenced the function as `this.event2Console`. This can be incredibly useful when you want to call the function from multiple places within the component. Both methods will produce the same result: a console log with our event object.

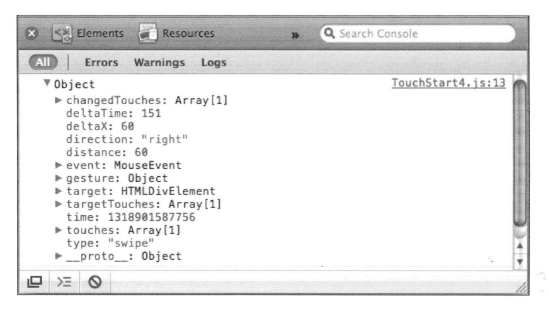

As you can see, we get a considerable amount of information from this event, including **direction**, **distance**, **deltaX**, **time**, and an event **type**. We can use this information as follows:

```
this.update(e.type+':'+e.direction+':'+e.distance);
```

This method can be added to our `this.event2Console` function, to update our panel with the type, direction, and distance of our swipe. Give it a try.

Also, play around with changing the `swipe` event in the code to any of the other functions in the list. Get a feel for what triggers each event and what information they return.

By using these touch events and the other events built into Sencha Touch, your program should be able to respond to just about any situation.

Additional information on events

The best place to get information about events is the Sencha Touch API docs at `http://docs.sencha.com/touch/1-1/`. Select a component in the list on the left, and look for the **Events** button at the top. You can click **Events** to go to the beginning of the section or hover your mouse pointer to see the full list of events and select a specific event from that list.

Clicking the down arrow next to the event will display a list of parameters for the event and any available examples on how the event can be used.

Another good place to find out about touch-specific events is the Kitchen Sink example application (`http://dev.sencha.com/deploy/touch/examples/kitchensink/`). Inside the application is a **Touch Events** section. This section allows you to tap or click on the screen to see which events are generated from the different taps and gestures.

The WebKit team at Sencha Touch has also created an event recorder for Android. You can get more information at `http://www.sencha.com/blog/event-recorder-for-android-web-applications/`.

Summary

In this chapter, we have covered a basic overview of events, and how to use listeners and handlers to get your program to respond to these events. We also covered a few of the more common events and took an in-depth look at `Ext.util.Observable`, which handles the events for every component in the Sencha Touch framework.

We talked about event delegation and the potential memory issues that can occur with listeners. We finished up the chapter with a look at touch-specific events and some tips on finding additional information about events.

In the next chapter, we will cover how to get and store data in Sencha Touch, using JSON, data stores, models, and forms.

6
Getting Data In

One of the key aspects of any application is the handling of data—getting data into the application so that you can manipulate and store it, and then getting it out again for display. We will spend the next two chapters covering data handling in Sencha Touch. This first chapter on data will focus on getting data into your application.

We will start with a discussion of the data models that are used to describe your data. We will then talk about readers that gather the data and the stores used to hold the data for use in our application. Once we have a grasp on where the data goes, we will cover how to use forms to get it there. We will look at how to validate your data and provide you with some examples of form submission. We will finish up with a look at getting the data back into a form for editing. This will serve as our starting point for the next chapter on data, which will cover getting data back for display.

This chapter covers the following topics:

- Data models
- Data formats
- Data stores
- Using forms and data stores

Models

The first step in working with data in a Sencha Touch application is to create a model of the data. If you are used to database-driven applications, it's helpful to think of the model as being a database schema: it's a construct that defines the data we are going to store, including the datatype, validations, and structure. This provides the rest of our application a common map for understanding the data being passed back and forth.

The basic model

At its most basic, the model describes the data fields using `Ext.regModel()`, such as:

```
Ext.regModel('User', {
  fields: [
    {name: 'firstname', type: 'string'},
    {name: 'lastname', type: 'string'},
    {name: 'username', type: 'string'},
    {name: 'age', type: 'int'},
    {name: 'email', type: 'string'},
    {name: 'active', type: 'boolean', defaultValue: true},
  ]
}
```

The first line declares that we have named our new model `User`. We then describe our data fields as an array of fields with a name, a type, and an optional default value. The name is simply how we want to refer to the data in our code. The valid datatypes are:

- `auto`: A default value that just accepts the raw data without conversion
- `string`: Converts the data into a string
- `int`: Converts the data into an integer
- `float`: Converts the data into a floating point integer
- `boolean`: Converts the data into a true or false Boolean value
- `date`: Converts the data into a JavaScript `Date` object

The default value can be used to set a standard value to be used, if no data is received for that field. In our example, we set the value of `active` to `true`. We can use this when creating a new user instance with `Ext.ModelMgr.create()`:

```
var newUser = Ext.ModelMgr.create({
  firstname: 'Nigel',
  lastname: 'Tufnel',
  username: 'goes211',
  age: 39,
  email: 'nigel@spinaltap.com'
}, 'User');
```

Notice that we did not provide a value for `active` in our new user instance, so it just uses our default value. This can also help when the user doesn't remember to enter in a value. We can also double-check the information our user enters by using `validations`.

Model validations

Model validations ensure that we are getting the data we think we are getting. These validations serve two functions. The first is to provide the guidelines for how data is entered. For example, we would typically want a username to consist only of letters and numbers; the validation can enforce this constraint and inform the user when they use the wrong character.

The second is security. Malicious users can also use the form field to send information that might potentially be harmful to our database. For example, sending DELETE * FROM users; as your username can cause problems if the database is not properly secured. It is always a good idea to validate data, just in case.

We can declare validations as part of our data model, in much the same way that we declare our fields. For example, we can add the following to our User model:

```
Ext.regModel('User', {
  fields: [
    {name: 'firstname', type: 'string'},
    {name: 'lastname', type: 'string'},
    {name: 'age', type: 'int'},
    {name: 'username', type: 'string'},
    {name: 'email', type: 'string'},
    {name: 'active', type: 'boolean', defaultValue: true},
  ],
  validations: [
    {type: 'presence',  field: 'age'},
    {type: 'exclusion', field: 'username', list: ['Admin', 'Root']},
     {type: 'length', field: 'username', min: 3},
    {type: 'format', field: 'username', matcher: /([a-z]+)[0-9]{2,3}/}
  ]
}
```

In our example, we have added four validations. The first one tests for the presence of an age value. If there is no value for age, we get an error. The second validator, exclusion, tests for things we don't want to see as a value for this field. In this case, we have a list of two items for username that we don't want to see: Admin and Root. The third validator tests to make sure that our value for username is at least three characters long. The final validator checks the format of our username using a regular expression.

> **Regular expressions**
>
> Regular expressions (also called **RegEx**) are an extremely powerful tool for matching the structure of a string. You can use RegEx to search for particular characters, words, or patterns, within a string. A discussion of regular expressions would require its own book, but there are a number of good online resources available.
>
>
>
> - Good tutorials are available at: http://www.zytrax.com/tech/web/regex.htm
>
> - A searchable database of regular expressions can be found at: http://regexlib.com
>
> - A wonderful regular expression tester is also available at: http://www.rexv.org/

We can test our validations by using the `validate` method on our new `User` instance:

```
var newUser = Ext.ModelMgr.create({
  firstname: 'Nigel',
  lastname: 'Tufnel',
  username: 'goes211',
  email: 'nigel@spinaltap.com'
}, 'User');

var errors = newUser.validate();
console.log(errors);
```

Notice that we intentionally dropped the `age` off this time, to give us an error. If we take a look at our console, we can see the error object that we get back:

```
▼Object                                          TouchStart.js:28
  allowFunctions: false
  ▶ events: Object
  ▼ items: Array[1]
    ▼ 0: Object
        field: "age"
        message: "must be present"
      ▶ __proto__: Object
    length: 1
    ▶ __proto__: Array[0]
  ▶ keys: Array[1]
    length: 1
  ▶ map: Object
  ▶ __proto__: Object
>
```

This is the console output for our `errors` object. The `errors` object includes a method called `isValid()`, which will return `true` or `false`. We can use this method to test for errors and return a message to the user, using something as follows:

```
if(!errors.isValid()) {
    alert("The field: "+errors.items[0].field+ " returned an error:
"+errors.items[0].message);
}
```

Here, we test for the length of our `errors` object. This will be zero if there are no errors. In this case, our `errors` object has a length of 1, so we grab the field that returned the error and the message it generated. These are included in the `items` list of the `errors` object. If there were more than one error, we would need to loop through the `items` list, to grab all of the errors.

We can also change the default error message by setting additional configuration options on the validations for:

- `exclusionMessage`: Used when we get an excluded value for a field
- `formatMessage`: Used when we get an improperly formatted value for a field
- `inclusionMessage`: Used when we do not get an included value for a field
- `lengthMessage`: Used when we get a value for a field that does not meet our required length
- `presenceMessage`: Used when we do not reserve a required value for a field

Customizing these errors will help the user understand exactly what went wrong and what needs to be done to correct the problem.

Model methods

Our models can also contain methods that can be called on any instance of our model. For example, we can add a method called `deactivate` to our model, by adding the following to our `User` model, after the `fields` list:

```
deactivate: function() {
  if(this.get('active')) {
   this.set('active', false);
  }
}
```

This function tests to see if our current value of `active` is `true`. If it is, we set it to `false`. Once we create our `newUser`, as we did previously, we can then call the function as follows:

```
newUser.deactivate();
```

These model methods provide a great way to implement common functions in your model.

CRUD

While model methods might look like a good place for adding functions to save our model, you really don't need to. These types of functions—`Create`, `Read`, `Update`, and `Destroy`—are often referred to by the unattractive acronym CRUD, and they are handled automatically by Sencha Touch. We will go over these functions a bit later in this chapter.

Now that we have our model's fields, validations, and functions defined, we need a way to pass data to and from the model for the storing and retrieving of our users. This is where the proxy and reader come in.

Proxies and readers

In the model, the proxy and reader form a partnership to store and retrieve data for use by the model. The proxy tells a model where its data will be stored, and the reader tells the model what format is being used to store the data.

There are two main types of proxies: local and remote. A local proxy stores its data locally on the device with one of three proxy types:

- `LocalStorageProxy` - Saves the data to local storage via the browser. This data is persistent across sessions, unless deleted by the user.

- `SessionsStorageProxy` - Saves its data to session storage via the browser. This data is removed when the session ends.

- `MemoryProxy` - This holds the data in local memory. When the page is refreshed, the data is deleted.

The remote proxy has two basic types:

- `AjaxProxy`: Sends requests to a server within the current domain

- `ScriptTagProxy`: Sends requests to a server on a different domain

For this chapter and the next, we will be dealing mostly with local proxies. We will cover remote proxies and synchronizing data in *Chapter 9, Advanced Topics*.

The proxy can be declared as part of the model, shown as follows:

```
proxy: {
  type: 'localstorage'
  id: 'userProxy',
}
```

All proxies require a type (local storage, session storage, and so on.), and some require a unique ID, so it's a good idea to just get into the habit of giving all of your proxies an ID.

We can also add a reader to this proxy configuration. The reader's job is to tell our proxy which format to use for sending and receiving data. The reader understands the following formats:

- `Array`: A simple JavaScript array.
- `XML`: Extensible Markup Language format.
- `JSON`: JavaScript Object Notation format.
- `JSONP`: JSON with padding. Typically used for communication with a remote server.

The reader gets declared as part of the proxy:

```
proxy: {
  type: 'localstorage',
  id: 'userProxy',
  reader: {
    type: 'json'
  }
}
```

Proxies and readers

Please note that the proxies and readers can also be declared as part of the data store and should ideally be declared in both places.

Introduction to data formats

Before we move on to data stores, we need to take a brief look at data formats. The three currently supported by Sencha Touch are Array, XML, and JSON. For each example, we will take a look at how the data would appear for a simple `contact` model with three fields: an ID, a name, and an e-mail.

Arrays

An `ArrayStore` data format uses a standard JavaScript array, which would look something such as this, for our `contact` example:

```
[
    [1, 'David', 'david@gmail.com'],
    [2, 'Nancy', 'nancy@skynet.com'],
    [3, 'Henry', 'henry8@yahoo.com']
]
```

One of the first things we notice about this type of array is that there are no field names included as part of a JavaScript array. This means if we want to refer to the fields by name in our template, we have to set up our model to understand where these fields should be mapped, by using the `mapping` configuration option:

```
Ext.regModel('Contact', {
    fields: [
        'id',
        {name: 'name', mapping: 1},
        {name: 'email', mapping: 2}
    ],
    proxy: {
      type: 'memory',
      reader: {
        type: 'array'
      }
    }
});
```

This sets up our `id` field as index 0 of our data, which is our default. We then use the `mapping` configuration to set `name` and `email` as index 1 and 2, respectively, of the items in our data array. We can then set the template values for the display component using the configuration:

```
itemTpl: '{name}: {email}'
```

While arrays are typically used for simple data sets, a larger or nested data set can become very unwieldy using the simple JavaScript array structure. This is where our other formats come in.

XML

XML or **Extensible Markup Language** should be a familiar looking format to anyone who has worked with HTML web pages in the past. XML consists of data nested within a series of tags that identify the name of each part of the dataset. If we put our previous example into XML format, it would look as follows:

```
<?xml version="1.0" encoding="UTF-8"?>
<contact>
<id>1</id>
<name>David</name>
<email>david@gmail.com</email>
</contact>
<contact>
<id>2</id>
<name>Nancy</name>
<email>nancy@skynet.com</email>
</contact>
<contact>
<id>3</id>
<name>Henry</name>
<email>henry8@yahoo.com</email>
</contact>
```

Notice that XML always begins with a version and encoding line. If this line is not set, the browser will not interpret the XML correctly and the request will fail.

We also include tags for defining the individual contacts. One advantage of this is that we can now nest data as shown:

```
<?xml version="1.0" encoding="UTF-8"?>
<total>25</total>
<success>true</success>
<contacts>
<contact>
<id>1</id>
<name>David</name>
<email>david@gmail.com</email>
</contact>
<contact>
<id>2</id>
<name>Nancy</name>
```

```
<email>nancy@skynet.com</email>
</contact>
<contact>
<id>3</id>
<name>Henry</name>
<email>henry8@yahoo.com</email>
</contact>
</contacts>
```

In this nested example, we have each individual `contact` tag nested inside a `contacts` tag. We also have tags for our `total` and `success` values.

Since we have a nested data structure, we will also need to let the reader know where to look for the pieces we need.

```
reader: {
    type: 'xml',
    root: 'contacts',
    totalProperty  : 'total',
    successProperty: 'success'
}
```

The `root` property tells the reader where to start looking for our individual contacts. We also set a value outside of our contacts list for `totalProperty`. This tells the store that there are a total of 25 contacts, even though the store only receives the first three. The `totalProperty` property is used for paging through the data (that is, showing three of 25).

The other property outside of our `contacts` list is `successProperty`. This tells the store where to look to see if the request was successful.

The only disadvantage of XML is that it's not a native JavaScript format, so it adds a little bit of overhead when it's parsed by the system. Typically, this is only noticeable in very large or deeply nested arrays, but it can be an issue for some applications.

Fortunately for us, we can also use JSON.

JSON

JSON or **JavaScript Object Notation** has all of the advantages of XML, but as a native JavaScript construct, it has less overhead associated with parsing. If we look at our data set as JSON, we would see the following:

```
[
  {
    "id": 1,
```

```
      "name": "David",
      "email": "david@gmail.com"
    },
    {
      "id": 2,
      "name": "Nancy",
      "email": "nancy@skynet.com"
    },
    {
      "id": 3,
      "name": "Henry",
      "email": "henry8@yahoo.com"
    }
  ]
```

We can also nest JSON in much the same way we do with XML:

```
{
  "total": 25,
  "success": true,
  "contacts": [
    {
      "id": 1,
      "name": "David",
      "email": "david@gmail.com"
    },
    {
      "id": 2,
      "name": "Nancy",
      "email": "nancy@skynet.com"
    },
    {
      "id": 3,
      "name": "Henry",
      "email": "henry8@yahoo.com"
    }
  ]
}
```

The reader would then be set up just as our XML reader, but with the type listed as JSON:

```
reader: {
    type: 'json',
    root: 'contacts',
    totalProperty  : 'total',
    successProperty: 'success'
}
```

As before, we set properties for both `totalProperty` and `successProperty`. We also provide the reader with a place to start looking for our `contacts` list.

JSONP

JSON also has an alternate format called JSONP, or JSON with padding. This format is used when you need to retrieve data from a remote server. We need this option because most browsers follow a strict same origin policy when handling JavaScript requests.

The same origin policy means that a web browser will permit JavaScript on the page to run as long as the JavaScript is running on the same server as the web page. This will prevent a number of potential JavaScript security issues.

However, there are times when you will have a legitimate reason for making a request from a remote server, say querying an API from a web service such as Flickr. Because your app isn't likely to be running on `flickr.com`, you'll need to use JSONP, which simply tells the remote server to encapsulate the JSON response in a function call.

Luckily, Sencha Touch handles all of that for us. When you set up your proxy and reader, set the proxy type to `scripttag`, and set your reader up like you would a regular JSON reader. This tells Sencha Touch to use `Ext.data.ScriptTagProxy` to do the cross-domain request, and Sencha Touch takes care of the rest.

 If you'd like to see JSONP and `Ext.data.ScriptTagProxy` in action, we use both to build the **Flickr Finder** application in *Chapter 8, The Flickr Finder Application.*

While we have a number of formats to choose from; we will be using the JSON format for all of our examples, moving forward, as we talk about data stores.

Introduction to stores

Stores, as the name implies, are used to store data. As we have seen in previous chapters, list components require a store in order to display data, but we can also use a store to grab information from forms and hold it for use anywhere in our application.

The store, in combination with the model and proxy, works in much the same way as a traditional database. The model provides the structure for our data (say a schema in a traditional database), and the proxy provides the communication layer to get the data in and out of the store. The store itself holds the data and provides a powerful component interface for sorting, filtering, saving, and editing data.

The store can also be bound to a number of components, such as lists, nested lists, select fields, and panels, to provide data for display.

We will cover display, sorting, and filtering in *Chapter 7, Getting Data Out*, but for now, we are going to look at saving and editing data with the store.

A simple store

As this chapter is concerned with getting data into the store, we are going to start out with a very simple local store for our example:

```
var contactStore = new Ext.data.Store({
  model: 'Contact',
  storeId: 'contactStore',
  proxy: {
    type: 'localstorage',
    id: 'myContacts',
    reader: {
      type: 'json'
    }
  },
    autoLoad: true
});
```

This example sets up the model for the store and then tells the proxy to store all the data as part of HTML5's local storage capability. We also set the store to `autoLoad`, which means that it will load the data as soon as the store is created.

We also need to set up our model correctly, in order to use this store. Even though we have the proxy listed as part of the store, it's a good idea to have it on the model as well. There will be times where we need to directly manipulate (update) the model, without getting the store first:

```
Ext.regModel('Contact', {
    fields: [
        {name: 'id', type:'int'},
        {name: 'name', type: 'string'},
        {name: 'email',  type: 'string'}
    ],
```

```
    proxy: {
        type: 'localstorage',
        id: 'myContacts',
        reader: {
          type: 'json'
        }
    },

});
```

This is our simple model with three items: an ID, a name, and an e-mail. We would then create a new contact as we did before:

```
var newContact = Ext.ModelMgr.create({
  name: 'David',
  email: 'david@msn.com'
  }, 'Contact');
```

Notice that we don't set the ID this time. We want the store to set that for us (similar to the way auto-increment works in a typical database). We can then add this new contact to the store and save it as this:

```
var addedUser = contactStore.add(newContact);
contactStore.sync();
```

The first line adds the user to the store, and the second line saves the contents of the store. By splitting out the add and sync functionalities, you can add multiple users to the store and then perform a single save, as the following:

```
var newContact1 = Ext.ModelMgr.create({
  name: 'David',
  email: 'david@msn.com'
  }, 'Contact');

var newContact2 = Ext.ModelMgr.create({
  name: 'Bill',
  email: 'bill@yahoo.com'
  }, 'Contact');

var addedContacts = contactStore.add(newContact1, newContact2);
contactStore.sync();
```

In both cases, when we add contacts to the store, we set up a return variable to grab the return value of the add method. This method returns an array of contacts, which will now have a unique ID as part of each `contact` object. We can take a look at these values by adding a couple of console logs after our sync:

```
console.log(addedContacts);
console.log(addedContacts[0].data.name+': '+addedContacts[0].data.id);
console.log(addedContacts[1].data.name+': '+addedContacts[1].data.id);
```

This will show that two `contact` objects in an array are returned. It also shows how to get at the data we need from those objects, by using the index number of the specific contact in the array. We can then drill down into the data for a name and the new ID that was assigned when we synced.

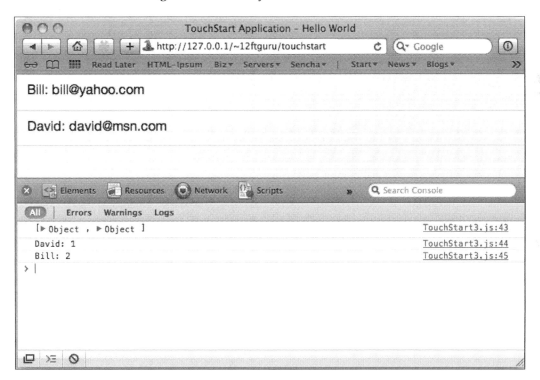

Now that we have a general idea of how to get data into a store, let's take a look at how to do it with a form.

Forms and stores

For this example, we are going to use the same store and model as our previous example, but we will add a list and a form, so that we can add new contacts and see what we have added. Let's start with the list:

```
this.viewport = new Ext.Panel({
    fullscreen: true,
    layout: 'fit',
    dockedItems: [{
        xtype: 'toolbar',
        dock: 'top',
        items: [{
            text: 'Add',
            handler: function() {
                addNewContact.show()
            }
        }]
    }],
    items: [
    {
      xtype: 'list',
      itemTpl: '{name}: {email}',
      store: contactStore
    }]
});
```

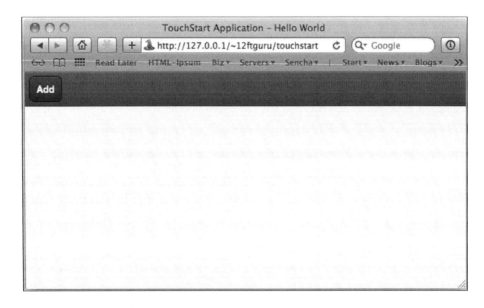

Most of the code here is pretty familiar from previous examples. We have a single panel with a `list` component. Our list has a template (`itemTpl`) that uses the same field names as our `contact` model and arranges how those will be displayed. We have also added a docked toolbar with our new **Add** button. The button has a very simple function that will show the `addNewContact` sheet, which we will create next:

```
var addNewContact = new Ext.Sheet({
    height: 250,
    layout: 'fit',
    stretchX: true,
    enter: 'top',
    exit: 'top',
    items: […]
});
```

This gives us our new sheet that will appear when we click the **Add** button. Now, we need to add our form fields to the `items` section of the sheet we just created:

```
{
    xtype: 'formpanel',
    padding: 10,
    id: 'contactForm',
    items: [
        {
            xtype: 'textfield',
            name : 'name',
            label: 'Full Name'
        },
        {
            xtype: 'emailfield',
            name : 'email',
            label: 'Email Address'
        }
    ]
}
```

We start by creating our `formpanel` component and then adding `textfield` and `emailfield` to the `items` list of `formpanel`. Make sure you include an `id` configuration on the form. This will allow us to get to it when we need to.

Specialty text fields

Sencha Touch uses specialty text fields, such as `emailfield`, `urlfield`, and `numberfield`, to control which keyboard is used by the mobile device, as in these iPhone examples:

The URL Keyboard   The Email Keyboard   The NumberKeyboard

- **The URL Keyboard** replaces the traditional Space bar with keys for dot (.), slash (/), and **.com**
- **The Email Keyboard** shortens the Space bar and makes room for @ and dot (.)
- **The Number Keyboard** initially presents the numeric keyboard instead of the standard QWERTY keyboard

These specialty fields do not automatically validate the data the user enters. Those kinds of validations are handled through model validations.

Specialty keyboards

Please note that Android and iOS have slightly different special keyboards, so you may find some variation between the two. It is usually helpful to run your application through both the Android and iOS simulators to ensure that the correct keyboard type is being used.

Mapping fields to the model

You will also notice that the name of each field in our form matches the name used by our `contact` model; this will allow us to easily create our contacts and add them to the store. However, before we get there, we need to add two buttons (**Save** and **Cancel**) to tell the form what to do.

After the `emailfield` object in our form, we need to add the following:

```
{
  xtype: 'button',
  height: 20,
  text: 'Save',
id: 'saveButton'
  margin: 10,
  handler: function() {
    this.up('sheet').hide();
  }
}, {
  xtype: 'button',
  height: 20,
  margin: 10,
  text: 'Cancel',
  handler: function() {
    this.up('sheet').hide();
  }
}
```

This gives us two buttons at the bottom of our form. Right now, both our **Save** button and our **Cancel** button do the same thing: they call a function to hide the sheet that holds our form. This is a good starting point, but we need a bit more to get our **Save** button to save our data.

Since we were good little coders and named our fields to match our model, we can just use the following code in our button handler to add our form to our store:

```
handler: function() {
  var form = this.up('form');
  var record = Ext.ModelMgr.create(form.getValues(), 'Contact');
  contactStore.add(record);
  contactStore.sync();
  form.reset();
  this.up('sheet').hide();
}
```

The first line uses the `up` method to grab the form that surrounds the button. Our second line uses `form.getValues()` and pipes the output directly into a new `Contact` model, using the `create()` method from our previous examples. We can then add the new contact to the store and sync, as we did before.

The last bit of cleanup we need to do is to clear all of the form values by using `form.reset()` and then hide the sheet, as before. If we don't reset the fields, the data would still be there the next time we showed the form.

The list connected to the store will refresh, when we sync the store, and our new contact will appear.

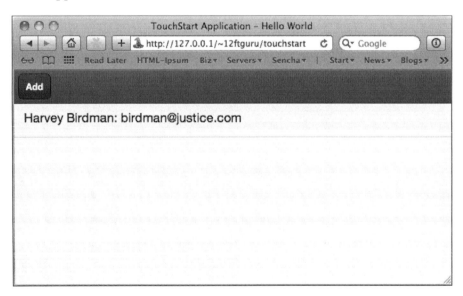

Since this store uses local storage for holding the data, our list will stay in place, even after we quit the Safari browser. This can be a bit of a pain when you are testing an application, so let's take a look at how to clear out the store.

Clearing store data

Local and session storage saves information on our local machine. Since we plan on doing lots of testing as we code, it's a good idea to know how to clear out this kind of data without removing other data that you might still need. To clear out the data for your local or session store, take the following steps:

1. Open up **Web Inspector** from the **Develop** menu and select the **Resources** tab.

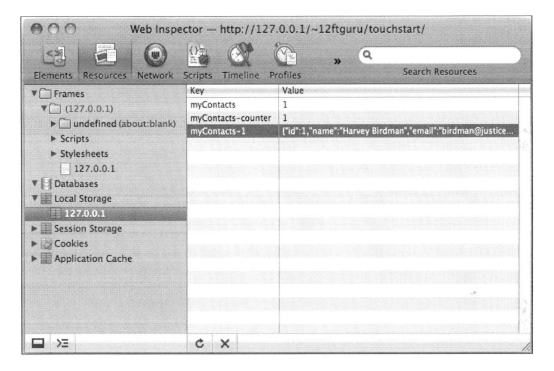

2. In the **Local Storage** or **Session Storage** section (depending on which method you use), you should see your application's database. Once you select the database, you can delete specific records or empty out the database completely. Just select the records on the right side of the screen, and click the **X** at the bottom to delete the record.

3. You can also reset the value for the counter by double-clicking on it and then changing the number. Be careful that you do not create multiple records with the same number. This will cause big problems.

4. Once you are finished in the **Resources** section, let's move on to editing data with our forms.

Editing with forms

Now that we have taken a look at the basics of getting data into a store, let's look at how to edit that data, using a few modifications to our current form.

The first thing we want to add is an `itemTap` listener on our list. This will let us tap an item in the list and bring up the form, with the selected entry included in the fields for us to edit. The listener looks like the following:

```
listeners: {
  itemTap: {
    fn: function(list,index){
      var rec = list.getStore().getAt(index);
      var form = Ext.getCmp('contactForm');
      form.load(rec);
      addNewContact.show()
    }
  }
}
```

Our `itemTap` listener will automatically get back a copy of the list and the index of the item that got tapped. We can then grab the store behind our list using `list.getStore()` and grab the tapped item using `getAt()` and the index value that was passed to us.

It is often useful to chain functions together in this fashion, especially if the piece you need only has to be used once. For example, we could have done:

```
var store = list.getStore();
var rec = store.getAt(index);
```

This would also let us use that `store` variable in a number of places within the function. Since we only need it to grab the record, we can do both of these lines as a single line:

```
var rec = list.getStore().getAt(index);
```

After we get the data record, we grab our form by using the ID of the form component and the `Ext.getCmp()` function. Now that we have the form, we can load the record and show the `addNewContact` sheet that contains our form.

As before, since we only use the form to do one thing, we could shorten the loading of the data record to the following:

```
Ext.getCmp('contactForm').load(rec);
```

We have included it here as two lines, just to show that either will work.

Now that the code is in place, you can tap any item in your list and see the edit form. This form looks exactly the same as before, but it now has the data, for the contact we clicked, filled in.

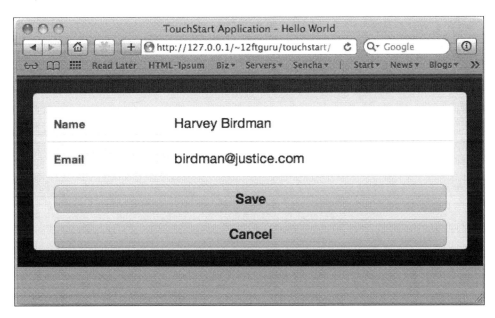

There's still one more problem to be dealt with; our **Save** button is hard coded to add a new record to the store. If we tap **Save** right now, we will just end up with multiple copies of the same contact. We need to make a change to our form, to let us switch what the **Save** button does, depending on whether we are editing or a creating new contact.

Switching handlers

In order to change the handler the button fires to save our contact, we need to separate the bulk of code from the button itself. To begin, locate the handler for our **Save** button, and copy the current function to your clipboard. Next, we want to replace that function with the name of an external function:

```
handler: addContact
```

Now, we have to create the new `addContact` function for this handler to use. In our JavaScript file, right before where we create our `addNewContact` sheet, add a new function called `addContact`, and paste in the code from our old `handler` function. It should look as follows:

```
var addContact = function() {
  var form = this.up('form');
  var record = Ext.ModelMgr.create(form.getValues(), 'Contact');
  contactStore.add(record);
  contactStore.sync();
  form.reset();
  this.up('sheet').hide();
};
```

This is the same old form-saving function we used on our button before, and it will work just fine for adding new contacts. Now, we need to create a similar function to update our contacts when we click on them in the list.

Up above our `addContact` function, add the following code:

```
var updateContact = function() {
  var form = this.up('form');
  var record = contactStore.getById(form.record.data.id);
  form.updateRecord(record);
  contactStore.sync();
  form.reset();
  this.up('sheet').hide();
};
```

This does almost the exact same thing as our other function. However, instead of grabbing the form fields and creating a new record, we grab the record from the store using `contactStore.getById()`. This record is the one we need to update with our new information.

We can find the ID for the record by looking at the form. Since we loaded the record into our form before we started editing, we can grab the ID we need with `form.record.data.id`.

Our record variable is now set to the old information from the data store. We can then pass that record to `form.updateRecord();`, which will overwrite the old information in the store record with our current form values. The ID will stay the same as we do not pass a new value for that.

After we update the record, we just sync, reset, and hide, as before.

Now that the code for our two functions is in place, we need to switch the handler for our **Save** button based on if the user clicked the **Add** button at the top of our list or selected an item in the list.

Let's start with the **Add** button. Locate the handler for our **Add** button at the top of our `list` object. We need to add some code to this button that will change the handler on the **Save** button:

```
handler: function() {
 var button = Ext.getCmp('saveButton');
 button.setHandler(addContact);
 button.setText('Create');
 addNewContact.show()
}
```

As our form button has a unique ID of `id: 'saveButton'`, we can grab it with `Ext.getCmp()` and make a few changes. The first is to update the handler to see our new `addContact` function, and the second is to change the text of the button to **Create**. We can then call `addNewContact.show()`, as before.

Our **Add** button is now set to show the form and change the text and handler for the button.

Now, we need to do something similar to the `tap` hander on our list:

```
itemTap: {
 fn: function(list,index){
  var rec = list.getStore().getAt(index);
  var form = Ext.getCmp('contactForm');
  form.load(rec);
  var button = Ext.getCmp('saveButton');
  button.setHandler(updateContact);
  button.setText('Update');
  addNewContact.show();
 }
}
```

Here, we still need to grab our data record and load it into the form, but now, we grab our `saveButton` method and make changes to the handler and text as well. The changes point the **Save** button to our `updateContact` function and change the text to `update`.

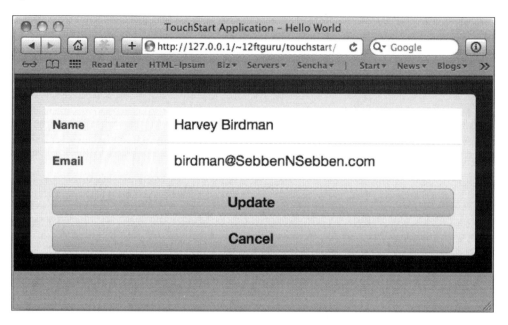

Deleting from the Data Store

If you remember earlier, when we talked about CRUD functions, you can see that we have successfully covered `Create`, `Read`, and `Update`. These are all handled automatically by the store with very little code required. What about `Delete`?

As it turns out, `Delete` is just as simple as our other store methods. We can use either of two methods: the first is `remove()` —it takes a record as its argument—and the second is `removeAt`, which takes an index to determine which record to remove. We could implement either of these as part of our edit form, by adding a new button at the bottom of the form, as this:

```
{
    xtype: 'button',
    height: 20,
    margin: 10,
    text: 'Delete',
    ui: 'decline',
```

```
handler: function() {
  var form = this.up('form');
  contactStore.remove(form.record);
  this.up('sheet').hide();
}}
```

Using `removeAt` requires the index of the store record, so we could do the same thing by changing the remove line to:

```
contactStore.removeAt(form.record.data.id);
```

That takes care of all of our basic `Create`, `Read`, `Edit`, and `Delete` functions. As long as you remember to set up your model and match your field names, the store will handle most of the basics automatically.

Further Information:

Sencha has a number of good tutorials on using forms and stores, including a video presentation located at `http://docs.sencha.com/touch/1-1/#!/video/26784522`.

You should also check out *Using the Data Package in Sencha Touch* at `http://www.sencha.com/learn/using-the-data-package-in-sencha-touch/`.

Summary

In this chapter, we covered the data model that forms the basic structure for all of our data in Sencha Touch. We looked at the proxy and reader, which handle communications between the data store and our other components. We also talked about the data store, which holds all of our data in Sencha Touch. Finally, we took a look at how you can use forms to get data in and out of the stores, as well as at how to delete the data when it is no longer needed.

In our next chapter, we will take a look at all of the other things we can do with data once we get it out of the store.

7
Getting Data Out

In the last chapter, we looked at how you can get data into a Sencha Touch data store. In this chapter, we will look at:

- Using data stores for display
- Binding, sorting, filtering, paging, and loading data stores
- Working with XTemplates
- Looping through data in an XTemplate
- Conditional display and inline functions in XTemplates
- Inline JavaScript and member functions in XTemplates
- Using Sencha Touch Charts to display store data

Using data stores for display

Being able to store data in your application is only half the battle. You need to be able to easily get the data back out and present it in a meaningful way to the user. Lists, panels, and other data-capable components in Sencha Touch offer three configuration options to help you accomplish this task: `store`, `data`, and `tpl`.

Directly binding a store

Dataviews, lists, nested lists, form select fields, and index bars are all designed to display multiple data records. Each of these components can be configured with a data store from which to pull these records. We introduced this practice earlier on in the book:

```
new Ext.Application({
name: 'TouchStart',
launch: function() {
```

```
Ext.regModel('Contact', {
fields: [
    {name: 'first', type: 'string'},
    {name: 'last', type: 'string'},
    {name: 'admin', type: 'boolean'}
  ]
});

this.viewport = new Ext.Panel({
fullscreen: true,
layout: 'fit',
items: [
    {
xtype: 'list',
itemTpl: '{last}, {first}',
store: new Ext.data.Store({
model: 'Contact',
storeId: 'contactStore',
proxy: {
type: 'localstorage',
id: 'myContacts',
reader: {
type: 'json'
      }
    },
autoLoad: true
    })
  }]
});

}
});
```

The store configuration takes model, storeId, and proxy components as part of its setup. This will grab all of the store's data and pull it into the list for display. This is pretty familiar to us now, but what if we only want some of the data, or if we need the data in a specific order?

As it turns out, Sencha Touch stores can be sorted and filtered both when they are first created and later, if we need to change the filtering or sorting in response to the user.

Sorters and filters

Sorters and filters can be used in a number of ways. The first way is to set up a default configuration on the store as part of its creation.

```
var myStore = new Ext.data.Store({
model: 'Contact',
  storeId: 'contactstore',
sorters: [
        {
property : 'lastLogin',
direction: 'DESC'
        },
        {
property :'first',
direction: 'ASC'
        }
    ],

filters: [
        {
property: 'admin',
value: true
        }
    ]
});
```

Our `sorters` component is set as an array of property and direction values. These are executed in order, so our example sorts first by `lastLogin` (most recent first); within `lastLogin`, we sort by name (alphabetically ascending).

Our filters are listed as `property` and `value` pairs. In our example, we want the store to show us `admin` only. The store might actually store non-admins as well, but here we are requesting that those be filtered out initially.

Sorters and filters can also be modified after the initial load-in by using one of the following methods:

- `clearFilter`: Clears all filters on the store, giving you the full content of the store.
- `filter`: Takes a filter object, just like the one in our previous configuration example, and uses it to limit the data as requested.

- `filterBy`: Allows you to declare a function that is run on each item in the store. If your function returns `true`, the item is included. If it returns `false`, then the item is filtered out.

- `sort`: Takes a `sort` object just like the ones in our configuration example and uses it to sort the data as requested.

If we use our previous example store, changing the `sort` order would look like this:

```
myStore.sort( {
property : 'last',
direction: 'ASC'
});
```

Filtering has to take into account any previous filters on the store. In our current store example, we are set to filter out anyone without an `admin` value of `true`. If we try the following code, we will not get back anything in the list, because we have effectively told the store to filter by both the new (`admin` = `false`) and previous (`admin` = `true`) filter:

```
myStore.filter( {
property : 'admin',
value: false
});
```

As `admin` is a Boolean value, we get back nothing. We have to clear out the old filter first:

```
myStore.clearFilter();
myStore.filter( {
property : 'admin',
value: false
});
```

This example will clear the old 'admin only' filter from the store and return a list of everyone who is not an admin.

Sorting and filters provide a powerful tool for manipulating data inside the data store. However, there are a few other situations we should also take a look at. What do you do when you have too much data, and what do you do when you need to reload the data store?

Paging a data store

In some cases, you will end up with more data than your application can comfortably manage in a single bite. For example, if you have an application with 300 contacts, the initial load-in time might be more than you really want. One way to handle this is with paging in the data store.

Paging allows us to grab the data in chunks and send the next or previous chunk of data, as the user needs it. We can set up paging using the `pageSize` configuration:

```
var myStore = new Ext.data.Store({
model: 'Contact',
storeId: 'contactStore',
proxy: {
type: 'localstorage',
id: 'myContacts',
reader: {
type: 'json'
        }
       },
autoLoad: true
     })
```

We can then move through the data using the paging functions:

```
myStore.nextPage();
myStore.PreviousPage();
myStore.loadPage(5);
```

This code moves forward one page, back one page, and then jumps to page five.

If we jump to page five and it doesn't exist, things will probably go poorly for our application (that is, it will go kaboom!). This means we need a good way to figure out how many pages we actually have, which means we need to know the total number of records in our data store.

We could try using the `getCount()` method for the data store, but this only returns the number of currently cached records in the store. Since we are paging through the data and not loading everything available, this would be the same as our maximum page size of 40. We need to set up our stores' reader to get this information.

We can set a configuration on the reader for `totalProperty`, such as this:

```
var myStore = new Ext.data.Store({
model: 'Contact',
storeId: 'contactStore',
    pageSize: 40,
```

```
proxy: {
type: 'localstorage',
id: 'myContacts',
reader: {
type: 'json'
        }
      },
autoLoad: true
      });
```

This tells our reader to look for an extra property, called `totalContacts`, in the data it collects. Our data that we pull into the store will also have to be set up to include this new property as part of the data string. How this is done will be determined largely by how your data is created and stored, but in a JSON data array, the format would look something like the following:

```
{
"totalContacts: 300,
  "contacts": [...]
}
```

All of our actual contacts would appear within the brackets, and the `totalContacts` property would be in the root of our array.

Once our data is set up in this fashion, we can grab the total contacts, as follows:

```
var total = myStore.getProxy().getReader().totalContacts
```

We can then divide by `myStore.pageSize`, to determine the total number of pages in our data. We can also grab the current page with `myStore.currentPage`. These two variables will allow us to display the users' current locations in the pages (that is, page five of eight).

One thing to be aware of, is that this total is not the number of records currently in the store. Instead, it is the total number of records available from the server. To find the total number of records in the store, you would use the following:

```
myStore.getCount();
```

Also, if you filter your stores' data, the number returned by `getCount()` will be the number of records that matched the filter, not the total number of records in the store.

Now, we need to account for what happens when the data behind our store changes.

Loading changes in a store

When we use a data store to pull from an external source, such as a file, a website, or a database, there is always the chance that the data will change at the external source. This will leave us with stale data in the store.

Fortunately, there is an easy way to deal with this using the `load()` function on the store. The `load()` function works as follows:

```
myStore.load({
scope: this,
callback: function(records, operation, success) {
console.log(records);
    }
});
```

The `scope` and `callback` functions are both optional. However, `callback` offers us an opportunity to do a number of interesting things, such as compare our old and new records, or alert the user visually once the new records are loaded.

Another consideration, when loading data stores, is whether to auto load the store as part of its creation or load it later. A good rule of thumb is to only auto load the data stores that you know will initially be displayed. Any subsequent stores can be set to load when the component they are bound to is shown.

For example, let's say we have a list of system users that will only be accessed occasionally within the program. We can add a listener to the component list itself, shown as follows:

```
listeners: {
show: {
fn: function(){ this.getStore().load(); }
    }
}
```

This code will load the store only if the `list` component is actually shown. Loading stores in this fashion saves us time when launching our application and saves memory.

We can also save time and memory by using the store to feed multiple components, such as a list of data and a details panel.

Data stores and panels

Unlike lists, where a number of records can be displayed, a panel typically displays a single record. However, we can still grab this information from our data store in the same way we do for a list.

Let's start with a variation of our contacts example from the beginning of the chapter; we will build a list of names using `first` and `last`, and then add a details panel that shows the full name, e-mail address, and phone number for the selected name.

We start with our model first:

```
Ext.regModel('Contact', {
fields: [
        {name: 'first', type: 'string'},
        {name: 'last', type: 'string'},
        {name: 'address', type: 'string'},
        {name: 'city', type: 'string'},
        {name: 'state', type: 'string'},
        {name: 'zip', type: 'string'},
        {name: 'email', type: 'string'},
        {name: 'birthday', type: 'date'}
    ]
});
```

This gives us our `first` and `last` values, which we will use for our initial list, and the `email`, `birthday`, and `address` information which we will use for the details.

Our `list` component stays basically the same as before. Since `list` uses the template `itemTpl: '{last}, {first}'`, it simply ignores the values for `address`, `city`, `state`, `zip`, `email`, and `birthday`. However, since these values are still part of the data record, we can still grab them and use them in our panel to display details.

Before we can add our panel, we need to change our `viewport` method over to use a `card` layout. This will let us switch between the list and the details with a single tap:

```
this.viewport = new Ext.Panel({
fullscreen: true,
layout: 'card',
id: 'cardStack',
activeItem: 0,
items: [
    {
xtype: 'list',
itemTpl: '{last}, {first}',
store: new Ext.data.Store({
```

```
model: 'Contact',
storeId: 'contactStore',
proxy: {
type: 'ajax',
url: 'api/contacts.json',
reader: {
type: 'json',
root: 'children'
        }
      },
autoLoad: true
    })
  }]
});
```

In this code, we have changed our original example to set the `viewport` method to a `card` layout, with the `activeItem` component as `0`. In this case, item `0` is our list. We also added an `id`, so we can grab the panel and change the active item later.

Sharp-eyed readers will also notice that we have changed our store to use AJAX as the proxy with a URL of `api/contacts.json`. This means that, when the store loads, it will look for a local file in the `api` folder, called `contacts.json`. This file will contain some test data we have thrown together, which looks something like the following:

```
{
  "children":[
    {
        "first":"Ila",
        "last":"Noel",
        "email":"ante.ipsum@Sedmalesuada.ca",
        "address":"754-6686 Elit, Rd.",
        "city":"Hunstanton",
        "state":"NY",
        "zip":34897,
        "birthday":"Tue, 16 Oct 1979 04:27:45 -0700"
    }, …
  ]
}
```

By setting this store to look at a local text file. This lets us add data quickly for testing, by adding additional new children to the text file.

Test data is your friend

Whenever you put together an application and test it, you will probably need some data in order to make sure things are working correctly. It's often very tedious to enter this information into a text file manually, or enter it in data forms over and over again. Fortunately, there is a website at http://www.generatedata.com/ that will generate random data in a number of formats. Just provide the field names and types, and then tell it how many records you need. Click the button, and you get back random data, ready for testing. Best of all, it's free.

Once you have your data and the new `viewport` set up, load the page to make sure things are working correctly.

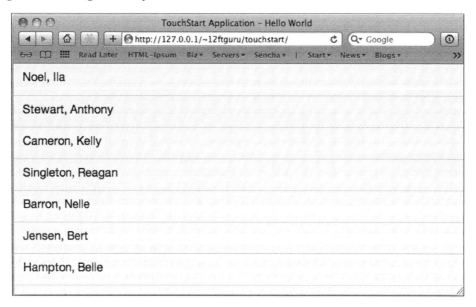

Now, we need to add data in our `detailsPanel` component. Let's start simple for this first part and add a new `panel` item after our list:

```
{
xtype: 'panel',
id: 'detailsPanel',
tpl: '{first} {last}<br>{address}<br>{city}, {state} {zip}<br>{email}<
br>{birthday}',
dockedItems: [{
xtype: 'toolbar',
dock: 'top',
items: [{
```

```
text: 'Back',
ui: 'back',
handler: function() {
Ext.getCmp('cardStack').setActiveItem(0);
}
}]
}]
}
```

Here, we just set `id` so we can grab the panel when we need to. We also add a simple template. We include some HTML line breaks to lay out the data better. Finally, we add a `Back` button which will bring us back to our main list.

The last thing we need to do is add a listener to our list to load the data into the panel:

```
listeners: {
itemTap: {
fn: function(list,index){
var record = list.getStore().getAt(index);
Ext.getCmp('detailsPanel').update(record.data);
Ext.getCmp('cardStack').setActiveItem(1);
}
}
}
```

The nice thing about this is that we don't really need to load anything new. The list already has access to all of the extra data through the data store. We just grab the store and use the `index` object that gets passed as part of our `itemTap` component. Then, we take the data from the `record` variable and pass it to the panel as part of the `update` function. Finally, we set the active item to our `detailsPanel` component. The result looks as follows, when we tap an item in the list:

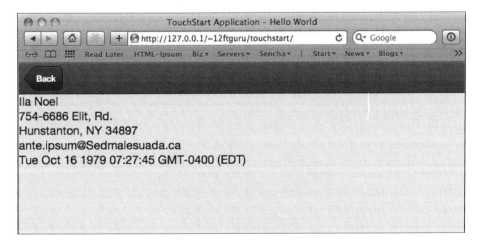

The `detailsPanel` component includes not only the first and last name from our list, but the address, e-mail, and birthday data, as well. All of this data comes from the same data store; we simply use the templates to choose which pieces to display.

Speaking of templates, ours looks a little bit dull, and the birthday is a bit more specific than we really need. There must be something we can do to dress this up a bit.

XTemplates

As we have seen from a number of previous examples, the **XTemplate** is a structure that contains HTML layout information and placeholders for our data.

So far, we have only created very basic templates for our list and panel, using the data values and a bit of HTML. We have also created them as part of the component itself, as a single string. This could become unwieldy very quickly. However, we can also set these templates up as separate components:

```
var myTemplate = new Ext.XTemplate(
  '{first} {last}<br>',
  '{address}<br>',
  '{city}, {state} {zip}<br>',
  '{email}<br>',
  '{birthday}'
);
```

This would create a template that looks exactly like what we had before. It's just a lot easier to read and maintain in this configuration. Here, we can have as many lines as we want, enclosed in quotes and separated by commas.

We can then add it to our panel with `tpl: myTemplate`.

This allows us to easily create something a bit more pretty than our old template:

```
var myTemplate = new Ext.XTemplate(
  '<div style="padding:10px;"><b>{first} {last}</b><br>',
  '{address}<br>',
  '{city}, {state} {zip}<br>',
  '<a href="mailto:{email}">{email}</a><br>',
  '{birthday}</div>'
);
```

This makes our display look a bit better.

We can also use these same types of XTemplates with our main list to give it a bit more style. For example, adding the following as the `itemTpl` component for our list will place an adorable kitten picture next to each name in the list:

```
var listTemplate = new Ext.XTemplate(
    '<div class="contact-wrap" id="{first}-{last}">',
    '<div class="thumb" style= "float: left;"><img src="http://
placekitten.com/36/36" title="{first}"></div>',
    '<span class="contact-name">{first} {last}</span></div>'
);
```

For this example, we just added some HTML to lay out each line of data and then used a random image generation service to place a 36 x 36 random kitten picture, which will line up next to our names on the left. (You can also use this to display the contact's picture).

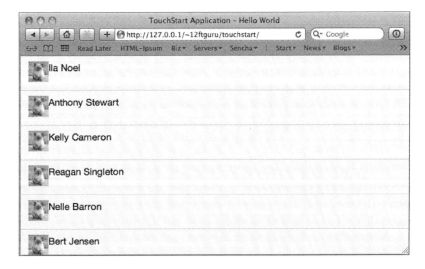

At this point, we are still just playing with basic HTML, but XTemplates are much more powerful than that.

Data manipulation

Since XTemplates are components in Sencha Touch, they allow us to directly manipulate the data within the template in a number of ways. The first thing we can do is clean up that ugly birthday.

Since the birthday is listed in our model as being a `date` object, we can treat it like one, in the template. We can replace the current birthday line of our template with the following:

```
'Birthday: {birthday:date("n/j/Y")}</div>'
```

This will use our value of `birthday` and the format function `date`. `date` uses the string `"n/j/Y"` to convert `birthday` into a more readable format. These format strings can be found on the date page of the Sencha Touch API.

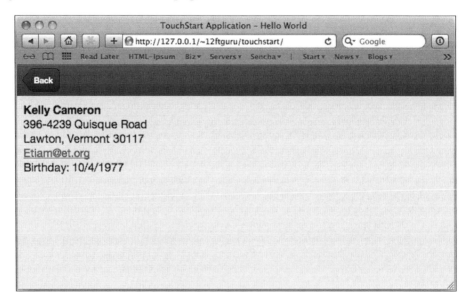

Sencha Touch includes a number of formatting functions that can be used in this fashion. Some of the functions include:

- `date`: Formats a `date` object using the specified formatting string (the format strings can be found on the date page of the Sencha Touch API).
- `ellipsis`: Truncates the string to a specified length and adds ... to the end (note that the ... is considered to be part of the total length).

- `htmlEncode` and `htmlDecode`: Converts HTML characters (&, <, >, and ') to and from HTML.

- `leftPad`: Pads the left side of the string with a specified character (good for padding numbers with leading zeros).

- `toggle`: A utility function that switches between two alternating values.

- `trim`: Removes any white space from the beginning and end of the string. It leaves spaces within the string intact.

The basic functions can be used inside the HTML of our XTemplate to format our data. However, the XTemplate has a few additional tricks up its sleeve.

Looping through data

In a list view, the XTemplate for the `itemTpl` component is automatically applied to each item in the list. However, you can also loop through your data manually, using the following syntax:

```
'<tpl for=".">',
'{name}</br>',
'</tpl>'
```

When you use the `<tpl>` tag, it tells the XTemplate we are exiting the realm of HTML and making some decisions within the template. In this case, `<tpl for=".">` tells the code to start a loop and use the root node of our data. The closing `</tpl>` tells the loop to stop.

Since we can have complex nested data with both XML and JSON, it can also be helpful to loop the data in places besides the root node. For example, let's say we have an array of states, and each state contains an array of cities. We could loop through this data as follows:

```
'<tpl for=".">',
'{name}</br>',

'<tpl for="cities">',
'{name}</br>',
'</tpl>'

'</tpl>'
```

Our first `<tpl>` tag begins looping through our states, printing the name. After the name is printed, it looks for a child array within the individual state, called `cities`.

This time, when we use the variable {name}, it's inside of our child loop, so it prints the name of each city in the state before moving on to the next state in the loop.

 Notice that, when we use a field name inside our `<tpl>` tags, we do not use the curly braces like this: {cities}. Since we are outside of the HTML piece of our template, Sencha Touch assumes "cities" is a variable.

We can even access an array nested in each city, for example postal codes, by adding another loop:

```
'<tpl for=".">',
'{name}</br>',

'<tpl for="cities">',
'{name}</br>',

'<tpl for="cities.postal">',
'{code}</br>',
'</tpl>'

'</tpl>'

'</tpl>'
```

In this case, we have used `<tpl for="cities.postal">` to indicate that we will loop through the postal codes data array within the cities data array. Our other array loops execute as before.

Numbering within the loop

When you are working inside a loop, it's often helpful to be able to count the cycles in the loop. You can do this by using {#} in your XTemplate:

```
'<tpl for=".">',
'{#} {name}</br>',
'</tpl>'
```

This will print the current loop number next to each name in the loop. This would work in a similar fashion for nested data:

```
'<tpl for=".">',
'{#} {name}</br>',

'<tpl for="cities">',
'{#} {name}</br>',
'</tpl>'

'</tpl>'
```

The first {#} will display where we are in the main loop and the second {#} will display where we are in the `cities` loop.

Parent data in the loop

In cases where we have nested data, it can also be helpful to be able to get to the parent properties from within the child loop. You can do this by using the `parent` object. Using our nested example with states, cities, and counties, this would look as follows:

```
'<tpl for=".">',
'{name}</br>',

'<tpl for="cities">',
'{parent.name} - {name}</br>',

'<tpl for="cities.postal">',
'{parent.name} - {code}</br>',
'</tpl>'

'</tpl>'

'</tpl>'
```

While inside our `cities` loop, {parent.name} would display the state name for that city. When we are inside our `cities.postal` loop, {parent.name} would display the city name associated with that postal code.

Using this {parent.fieldname} syntax, we can get to any of the parent's values from within the current child item.

Conditional display

In addition to looping, XTemplates offer some limited conditional logic for use in your template. This is limited because, instead of the familiar programming concept of `if...else...then`, Sencha Touch only offers `if...then`. For example, we could use the `if` statement in our states and cities to only display cities with a population above 2,000:

```
'<tpl for=".">',
  '{name}</br>',
  '<tpl for="cities">',
    '<tpl if="population &gt; 2000">',
      '{name}</br>',
    '</tpl>',
  '</tpl>',
'</tpl>'
```

If we wanted to color code our cites based on whether they are over or under our population target, then we couldn't use if... else... then. We would have to do it as two opposite if statements:

```
'<tpl for=".">',
  '{name}</br>',
  '<tpl for="cities">',
    '<tpl if="population &gt; 2000">',
      '<div class="blue">{name}</div>',
    '</tpl>',
    '<tpl if="population &lt; 2000">',
      '<div class="red">{name}</div>',
    '</tpl>',
  '</tpl>',
'</tpl>'
```

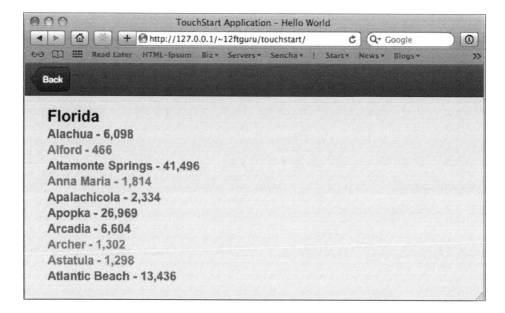

Now, you are probably already asking yourself why we are using > and < instead of > and <. The reason is because anything in our conditional statement needs to be HTML-encoded, in order for the XTemplate to correctly parse it. This can be a bit confusing at first, but the key things to remember are as follows:

- Use > instead of >.
- Use < instead of <.

- Use equals as normal `==` However, if you are comparing a string value, you have to escape the single quotes such as this: `'<tpl if="state == \'PA\'">'`.

- You will need to encode `"`, if it is part of your conditional. So if you are searching for the word `"spam"` including the quotes, you would have to encode this `as&quot;spam&quot;`.

Arithmetic

In addition to conditional logic, the XTemplates also support basic math functionality for the following:

- Addition (+)
- Subtraction (-)
- Multiplication (*)
- Division (/)
- Modulus—the remainder of one number divided by another (%)

For example:

```
'<tpl for=".">',
  '{name}</br>',
  '<tpl for="cities">',
      '{name}</br>',
  'Population: {population}</br>',
  'Projected Population for next year: {population * 1.15}</br>',
  '</tpl>',
'</tpl>'
```

This would give us our initial population value followed by a projected population of 1.15 times the current population. The math functions are included within the curly braces around our variable.

Inline JavaScript

We can also execute arbitrary inline code as part of our Xtemplate. We can do this by placing the code within a combination of brackets and curly braces: { [...] }. There are also a few special attributes we can access within this code:

- `values`: The values in the current scope
- `parent`: The values of the current parent object

- xindex: The current index of the loop you are on
- xcount: The total number of items in the current loop

For example, we can make sure our state and city names are uppercase, and alternate colors on our list of cities with the following XTemplate:

```
'<tpl for=".">',
  '{[values.name.toUpperCase()]}</br>',
  '<tpl for="cities">',
  '<div class="{[xindex % 2 === 0 ? "even" : "odd"]}">',
      '{[values.name.toUpperCase()]}</br>',
  '</div>',
  '</tpl>',
'</tpl>'
```

In this case, we use {[values.name.toUpperCase()]} to force the name of the state and the city to be uppercase. We also use {[xindex % 2 === 0 ? "even" : "odd"]} to alternate our row colors, based on the remainder of the current count divided by 2 (the modulus).

Even with the ability to write inline JavaScript, there are a number of cases where you might require something a bit more robust. This is where the XTemplate member functions come into play.

XTemplate member functions

An XTemplate member function allows you to attach a JavaScript function to your XTemplate and then execute it inside the template by calling this.function_name.

The functions are added to the end of the template and a template can include multiple member functions. These member functions are wrapped in a set of curly braces in a fashion similar to listeners:

```
{
myTemplateFunction: function(myVariable) {
   ...
 },
myOtherTemplateFunction: function() {
   ...
 }
}
```

We can use these member functions to make up for the lack of a native if...then... else option within the template. Let's use our previous states and cities example, and expand our color coding a bit.

```
'<tpl for=".">',
  '{name}</br>',
  '<tpl for="cities">',
      '<div class="{[this.setPopulationStyle(values.
population)]}">{name}</div>',
    '</tpl>',
  '</tpl>',
'</tpl>',
{
setPopulationStyle: function(population) {
if(population >= 4000) {
return 'red';
  } else if(population <= 3999 && population >= 2000) {
return 'orange';
  } else if(population <= 1999&& population >= 1000) {
return 'blue';
  } else {
return 'grey';
  }
 }
}
```

For this example, we have created a member function called `setPopulationStyle`, that we pass our population variable into. As our function can execute any JavaScript we desire, we can use our `if...then...else` logic here, setting a class for our population in the template. We can then call the function inside our template with `{[this. setPopulationStyle(values.population)]}`, which will print out our class name, based on the value of our population.

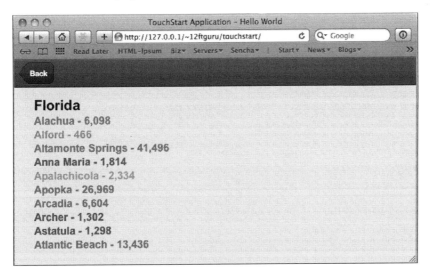

We can also use our member functions to help us test for the presence or absence of data. This comes in very handy for controlling your template. For example, let's start with a contacts template with a name, address, and e-mail, such as the following:

```
var myTemplate = new Ext.XTemplate(
  '<div style="padding:10px;"><b>{first} {last}</b><br>',
  '{address}<br>',
  '{city}, {state} {zip}<br>',
  '<a href="mailto:{email}">{email}</a><br>',
  'Birthday: {birthday:date("n/j/Y")}</div>'
);
```

If we have no data for the address, city, and state, we will end up with some empty lines and a stray comma. Since our `zip` variable is an integer according to our model, it will show up as **0** if we don't have a value stored for it.

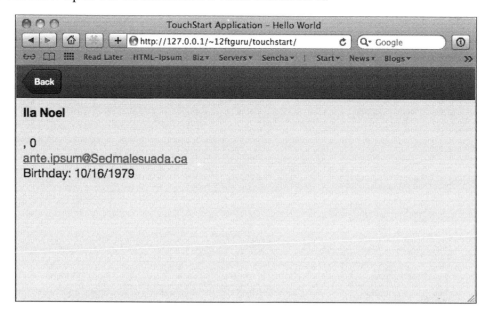

We need a way to check and see if we have data for these items before we print it out.

isEmpty

As it turns out, native JavaScript is very problematic when it comes to detecting an empty value. Depending on the function, JavaScript might return the following:

- null
- undefined

- an empty array
- an empty string

For most of us, these are pretty much the same thing; we didn't get back anything. However, to JavaScript, these return values are very different. If we try to test for data with if(myVar == '') and we get back null, undefined, or an empty array, JavaScript will return false.

Fortunately, Sencha Touch has a handy little function called isEmpty(). This function will test for null, undefined, empty arrays, and empty strings, all in one function. However, Sencha Touch does not have an opposite function for has data, which is what we really want to test for. Thanks to template member functions, we can write our own.

```
var myTemplate = new Ext.XTemplate(
  '<div style="padding:10px;"><b>{first} {last}</b><br>',
  '<tpl if="!Ext.isEmpty(address)">',
  '{address}<br>',
  '{city}, {state} {zip}<br>',
  '</tpl>',
  '<a href="mailto:{email}">{email}</a><br>',
  'Birthday: {birthday:date("n/j/Y")}</div>'
```

We don't even need a member function for this data check. We can add <tpl if="!Ext.isEmpty(address)"> to our template and check for the address in line with our template. The Ext.isEmptyfunction class takes the address data and checks to make sure it is not ! (empty). If the address is not empty, we print the address and if it is empty, we do nothing.

Changing a panel's content with XTemplate.overwrite

In our previous examples, we have declared our XTemplate as part of our panel or list, using tpl or itemtpl. However, it can also be helpful to overwrite a template programmatically, after the list or panel is displayed. You can do this by declaring a new template and then using the panel's (or list's) overwrite command to combine the template and the data, and overwrite the content area of your panel or list.

```
var myTemplate = new Ext.XTemplate(
'<tpl for=".">',
  '{name}</br>',
  '<tpl for="cities">',
      '- {name}<br>',
    '</tpl>',
```

```
    '</tpl>',
'</tpl>'
);

myTemplate.overwrite(panel.body, data);
```

Our `overwrite` function takes an element (`Ext` or `HTML`) as the first argument. So, instead of just using panel, we need to use the body element of the panel as `panel.body`. We can then supply a record from a data store or an array of values, as our second argument for the new template to use.

While XTemplates are an extremely powerful way to display our data, they are still very text heavy. What if we want to display data as something a bit more colorful? Let's take a look at Sencha Touch Charts.

Sencha Touch Charts

So far, we have only looked at data stores and records as a way to display text data, but with the release of Sencha Touch Charts, we are a now able to display complex graphical data as part of our applications.

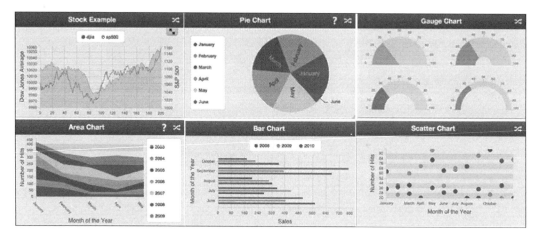

These new components use data stores to display a wide range of chart and graph types, including the following:

- pie
- bar
- line
- scatter

- series

- treemap

- worldmap

While a full exploration of the chart components would be worthy of a book by itself, we want to provide an overview of how these components interact with the data store and, hopefully, peak your curiosity.

Installing Touch Charts

Sencha Touch Charts are a separate download from the main Sencha Touch framework, and you can find them at `http://www.sencha.com/products/touch/charts/`.

You will need to unzip the `touch-charts` folder and move it into your folder, much in the same way we set up our Sencha Touch framework in *Chapter 2, Creating a Simple Application*. You will also need to include the `touch-charts-debug.js` and `touch-charts-demo.css` files in your main `index.html` file (both files are in the `touch-charts` folder). Follow the previous instructions in *Chapter 2, Creating a Simple Application*, for including JavaScript files.

A simple pie chart

Once the files are included, we can start a new JavaScript file for our Charts example. We will start with a data store:

```
Ext.setup({
onReady: function() {
var mystore = new Ext.data.JsonStore({
fields: ['month', 'sales'],
data: [
        {'month': 'June', 'sales': 500},
        {'month': 'July', 'sales': 350},
        {'month': 'August', 'sales': 200},
        {'month': 'September', 'sales': 770},
        {'month': 'October', 'sales': 170}
    ]
  });
 }
});
```

Our store declares two field types, month and sales, and our data array holds five sets of month and sales values. This will feed into our pie chart:

```
var chartPanel = new Ext.chart.Panel({
title: 'Pie Chart',
fullscreen: true,
items: {
cls: 'pie1',
theme: 'Demo',
store: mystore,
insetPadding: 20,
legend: {
position: {
portrait: 'bottom',
landscape: 'left'
}
},
series: [{
type: 'pie',
field: 'sales',
showInLegend: true,
label: {
field: 'month'
}
}]
}
});
```

Much like our other panel components, an Ext.chart.Panel class takes configurations for title and fullscreen. It also takes a list of items to include in the body of the panel. In the case of a chart panel, this item will be a single chart component.

The chart component takes configurations options for cls (a CSS class), a theme, a data store component, and insetPadding component to keep the chart from bumping up against the top and sides of the page.

Next, we have a configuration for our legend chart. This provides a color-coded reference for all of our chart values. We can use a position configuration to designate how the legend should appear in both portrait and landscape modes.

The final piece is our series configuration. In our example, we have set the type of chart we will see, which field the chart uses to draw the pie slices, whether to show the legend or not, and lastly, the label we will use for our legend.

The series configuration

The series configuration controls most of the look and feel of our charts: shadows, animation handling, gradients, as well as the actual type of chart we want (pie, column, bar, scatter, and so on). A series will be composed of an array of items that control the positioning of each of our chart elements as well as the value from our store that we are using for that element. This also means that each type of chart will have a slightly different set of requirements and options for its series data. Consult the API Drawing and Charting documentation to see examples of the different types of series configurations: `http://docs.sencha.com/touch-charts/1-0/#!/guide/drawing_and_charting`.

When we load it all up, our chart looks as follows:

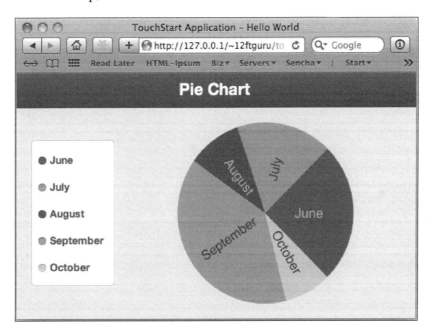

If you click on any of the months on the legend, you can turn them on and off in the chart. This functionality happens automatically, without any additional code.

A pie chart works well for very simple, single-series data, but what happens if we have data for several years? Let's see how a bar chart might work to display this kind of data.

A bar chart

For our bar chart, let's replace our chart data store with this one:

```
var mystore = new Ext.data.JsonStore({
fields: ['month', 'data'],
data: [
  {'month': 'June', '2008': 500, '2009': 400, '2010': 570},
  {'month': 'July', '2008': 350, '2009': 430, '2010': 270},
  {'month': 'August', '2008': 200, '2009': 300, '2010': 320},
  {'month': 'September', '2008': 770, '2009': 390, '2010': 670},
  {'month': 'October', '2008': 170, '2009': 220, '2010': 360}
]
});
```

This data set has multiple series of data we need to display (five months, with three years for each month). An effective bar chart will need to display a row for each month and separate bars within the month for each of our years.

We can start by changing the title of our chart panel to *bar chart*. Then, we can replace our chart items, as follows:

```
items: {
cls: 'bar1',
theme: 'Demo',
store: mystore,
animate: true,
legend: {
position: {
portrait: 'right',
landscape: 'top'
        },
labelFont: '17px Arial'
    },
axes: [{
type: 'Numeric',
position: 'bottom',
fields: ['2008', '2009', '2010'],
title: 'Sales',
minimum: 0
    },
    {
type: 'Category',
position: 'left',
fields: ['month'],
```

```
title: 'Month of the Year'
  }],
series: [{
type: 'bar',
xField: 'month',
yField: ['2008', '2009', '2010'],
axis: 'bottom',
showInLegend: true
  }]
}
```

Like our pie chart, the bar chart component takes configurations options for `cls` (a CSS class), a `theme`, a data `store`, and new option called `animate`. This option will make our bars animate as we turn on and off different items in the legend.

We then have our legend as before, followed by a new configuration option called `axes`. Since a bar chart operates along an X and a Y axis, we need to specify which of our data points should feed each axis.

First up is our sales data for each year. The data is numeric, positioned along the bottom and given a title of `sales`. We also specify the fields that will be used for this access and what our minimum value should be (this is the number that will appear on the far left of our bar chart and will usually be zero).

The next axis is our category data (which will also be used for our legend). In this case, our `position` is `left`, our `field` is `month`, and our `title` is `Month of the Year`. This closes out our `axes` configuration.

Finally, we have our `series` configuration, which sets this up as a bar graph. Unlike our previous pie chart example, which only tracked sales data, the bar chart is tracking sales data for two separate points (`month` and `year`), so we need to assign our `xField` and `yField` variables and declare an axis location. This location should match the axis where you are displaying numerical data (in our case, the data is on the Y axis, which is on the bottom). We close out by using `showInLegend` to display our legend.

The final chart should look as follows:

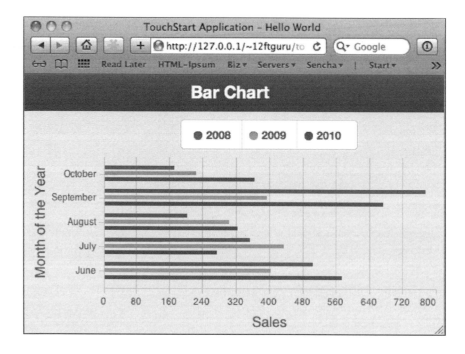

 Charts are an incredibly robust way to use stores to display data, and we don't really have time to go through them all here, but you can explore all of the capabilities of Sencha Charts at http://www.sencha.com/products/touch/charts/.

You can also find examples of each kind of chart at http://dev.sencha.com/deploy/touch-charts-1.0.0/examples/. Remember that you need to view these examples with a WebKit browser (Safari or Chrome).

The full Touch Charts API documentation is available at http://docs.sencha.com/touch-charts/1-0/.

Summary

In this chapter, we have explored the way data stores can be used to display both simple and complex data. We talked about binding, sorting, paging, and loading data stores. We then walked through using data stores with both lists and panels.

We covered how to lay out your application by using XTemplates to control how the data from stores and records will appear. We explored how to manipulate and loop through our data inside an XTemplate as well as how to use conditional logic, arithmetic, and inline JavaScript. We finished up our conversation on XTemplates by discussing member functions and some of their uses.

We closed out our chapter with a look at using the Sencha Touch Charts package to display our store data graphically.

In our next chapter, we will explore putting all of the information from our previous chapters together into a full-scale application.

The Flickr Finder Application

8

So far, we have looked at Sencha Touch components individually or in small, simple applications. In this chapter, we are going to create a well-structured and more detailed application, using Sencha Touch. This will include:

- An introduction to the **Model View Controller** (**MVC**) design pattern
- Setting up a more robust folder structure
- Setting up the main application files
- Using the Flickr API
- Registering components
- Setting up the SearchPhotos component
- Setting up the SavedPhotos component
- Adding the finishing touches to publish the application

The basic application

The basic idea for this application will be to use the Flickr API to discover photos taken near our location. We will also add the ability to save interesting photos we might want to look at later.

When you are first creating an application, it's always a good idea to sketch out the interface. This gives you a good idea of the pieces you will need to build and also allows you to navigate through the various screens the way a user would. It doesn't need to be pretty; it just needs to give you a basic idea of all the pieces involved in creating the application.

Aim for something very basic, such as this:

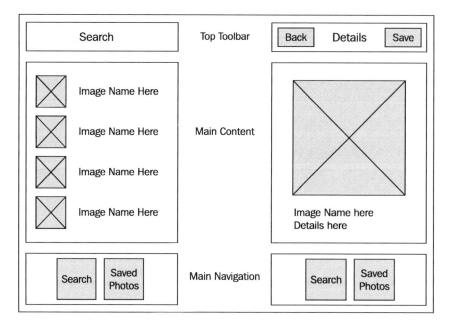

Next, you will want to tap your way through the paper interface, just like you would with a real application, and think about where each tap will take the user, what might be missing, and what might be confusing for the user.

Our basic application needs to be able to display a list of photos as well as a close-up of a single photo. When we tap a photo in the list, we will need to show the larger close-up photo. We will also need a way to get back to our list when we are finished.

When we see a photo we like, we need to be able to save it, which means we will need a button to save the photo as well as a separate list of saved photos and a close-up single view for the saved photo, as well.

Once we are happy with the drawings, we can start putting together the code to make our paper mock-up into something like this:

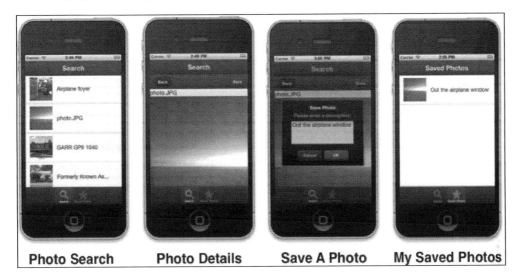

| Photo Search | Photo Details | Save A Photo | My Saved Photos |

Introduction to Model View Controller (MVC)

Before we get started building our application, we should spend some time talking about structure and organization. While this might seem like a boring detour into application philosophy, it's actually one of the most critical considerations for your application.

First consider the monolithic application, with everything in one enormous file. It seems crazy, but you will encounter hundreds of applications that have been coded in just this fashion. Attempting to debug something such as this is a nightmare. Imagine finding the missing closing curly brace inside of a component array 750 lines long. Yuck!

The question then becomes one of how to break up the files in a logical fashion.

Model View Controller, or MVC, organizes the application files based on the functionality of the code:

- Models describe your data and its storage
- Views control how the data will be displayed
- Controllers handle the user interactions by taking input from the user and telling the views and model how to respond, from the user's input

This means each part of your application will have separate files for each of these parts. Let's take a look at how this is structured:

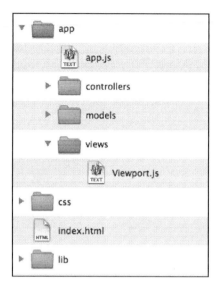

Our **css** folder contains our local style sheets and our **lib** folder contains our Sencha Touch library files, just as before, but we have some new folders named **models**, **controllers**, and **views**, inside our **app** folder.

Our **model** files will contain code for creating our models and the stores that will contain our data. There will be one model file for each of our different datatypes (we will talk about how to split out the datatypes in the next section).

Our **controller** files will contain most of the functionality for the application: loading the data into the store, getting the data back out for display, and listening for any input from the user. These controller files will also be split into separate files for each type of data that we deal with.

The **views** folder will contain all of our display information for each of our data pieces. Since we will likely have multiple views for each of our datatypes (for example, a form and a list), we will probably split these views out into separate sub folders, one per datatype.

By splitting the files out this way, it is much easier to reuse code across applications. For example, let's say you build an application that has a model, controller, and views for a user. If you want to create another application that needs to deal with users, you can simply copy over the individual files for the model, views, and controller into your new application. If all the files are copied over, then the user code should work just as it did in the previous application.

If we build a monolithic application, you would have to hunt though the code and grab out bits and pieces, and reassemble them in the new application. This would be a slow and painful process. By separating our components by functionality, it's much easier to reuse code between projects.

Building the foundation

Before we can build the application, we need to set up our HTML file that will link to the rest of our files and serve as the overall container for our application:

```
<!doctype html>
<html>
<head>
<meta http-equiv="Content-Type" content="text/html; charset=utf-8">
<title>Flickr Findr</title>

<meta name="viewport" content="width=device-width, user-scalable=no,
initial-scale=1.0; maximum-scale=1.0; user-scalable=0;" />
<meta name="apple-mobile-web-app-capable" content="yes" />
<link rel="apple-touch-icon" href="apple-touch-icon.png" />

<link rel="stylesheet" href="lib/resources/css/sencha-touch.css"
type="text/css">
<link rel="stylesheet" href="css/flickrfindr.css" type="text/css">
</head>
<body>
<script type="text/javascript" src="lib/sencha-touch-debug.js"></
script>

<div id="sencha-app">
<script type="text/javascript" src="app/app.js"></script>

<!-- Place your view files here -->
<div id="sencha-views">

</div>

<!-- Place your model files here -->
<div id="sencha-models">

</div>

<!-- Place your controller files here -->
<div id="sencha-controllers">
```

```
    </div>
    </div>
    </body>
    </html>
```

This basic HTML file setup links to all of our various JavaScript files and the Sencha Touch framework. In the body of the `index.html` file, we have also created three sections for our model, view, and controller files. As you create each file, you will need to add a link to the file in the appropriate section of the index file.

Placing models, views, and controllers in the page body

In a typical HTML page, JavaScript is placed in the `<head></head>` tags. When the browser loads that page, it must load everything in the head tag before loading the rest of the page. Once the head tag is fully loaded, any HTML within the `<body></body>` tags gets rendered, and any files in the body tags are loaded serially. By moving our components inside the `<body></body>` tag, we can load the pieces the user will see first, at the top of our list. This leads to a slightly quicker load time from the user's perspective.

Next, we need a way to launch the initial application, and a basic structure where we can place our different data views for display.

This foundation begins with two files: one called `viewport.js`, in the `views` folder, and another called `app.js`, in the main `app` folder. Let's take a look at these files.

The code for our `app.js` file is pretty simple:

```
FlickrFindr = new Ext.Application({
defaultTarget: "viewport",
name: "FlickrFindr",
launch: function() {
this.viewport = new FlickrFindr.Viewport();
    }
});
Ext.namespace('FlickrFindr.view', 'FlickrFindr.model', 'FlickrFindr.
store', 'FlickrFindr.controller');
```

This is the file that initially declares our `viewport` method and launches our application. We also create the initial namespace for our models, views, and controllers. As we mentioned back in *Chapter 2, Creating a Simple Application*, namespace makes sure that when I call `FlickrFinder.Viewport()`, I don't end up getting the generic `Ext.Viewport` instead.

Namespace bug

There is currently a namespace bug in Sencha Touch 1.1, in the Ext. Application setup. Currently, as stated in the documentation, when the application is created, Ext calls the ns function to create the namespaces we need for our application. Unfortunately, the function ns does not actually exist in version 1.1 of Sencha Touch, so the namespaces are not created automatically. The upshot of this is that we have to create them manually (no matter what the Sencha Touch 1.1 documentation might tell you).

The launch function creates our new FlickrFindr.Viewport() method, which we will define in our viewport.js file.

As before, our viewport is simply an extension of a standard Ext.Panel component. In the viewport.js file, add the following:

```
FlickrFindr.Viewport = Ext.extend(Ext.Panel, {
layout    : 'card',
fullscreen: true,

initComponent: function() {
Ext.apply(this, {
items: [
{ xtype: searchphotos }
]
        });

FlickrFindr.Viewport.superclass.initComponent.apply(this, arguments);
    }
});
```

This viewport will be the skeleton of our application, which will hold our other components. However, unlike our previous examples, the bulk of our individual component code is going to live in separate files. Our items section lists a single component with an xtype attribute of searchphotos. We will create this component in the *The SearchPhotos component* section.

Splitting up the pieces

The next thing we need to consider is how our application gets split into our separate MVC pieces. For example, if your application tracks people and what car they own, you would likely have a model and controller for the people, and a separate model and controller for the cars. You would also likely have multiple views for both cars and people, such as add, edit, list, details, and so on.

In our application, we will be dealing with two different types of data. The first is our search data for our photos and the second is our saved photos.

If we break this down into models, views, and controllers, we get something such as the following:

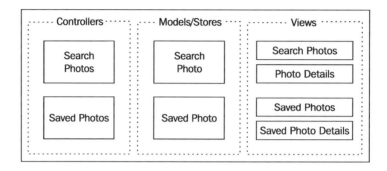

Our controllers are separated out by functionality for saved photos and search photos.

Since they are dealing with the same type of data, each of our controllers can use the same model, but they will need different stores, since they're each using different actual data sets. Our data stores will be part of the model file, so we have left the two models as separate blocks in our diagram (since they will still be separate files).

For views, our search needs a list view for **Search Photos** and a **Photo Details** view. The saved photos will also need a view for the list of saved photos and a view for editing/adding the saved photos.

Naming conventions

There are a few naming conventions when you use an MVC structure. While they are not required, they are strongly recommended. The conventions will make it easier to understand for anyone else who has to work with your code. The controller is typically a plural word or words. A model is a singular version of the controller name. Finally, the default view for the controller should be named the same (remember, the models, views, and controllers are in separate folders). This will make it clear which pieces belong together within your code.

Now that we have an idea of how our application needs to be laid out, we have one last task to perform before we get started. We need to get an API key from Flickr.

Using the Flickr API

A majority of popular web applications have made an **API** (**Application Programming Interface**) available for use in other applications. This API works in much the same way as our Sencha Touch framework. The API provides a list of methods that can be used to read from, and even write data to, the remote server.

These APIs typically require a key in order to use them. This allows the service to keep track of who is using the service and curtail any abuses of the system. API keys are generally free and easy to acquire.

Go to the Flickr API site, `http://www.flickr.com/services/api/`, and look for the phrase **API Keys**. Follow the link and apply for an API key, using the form provided. When you receive your API key, it will be a 32-character long string composed of numbers and lowercase letters.

Each time you send a request to the Flickr API server, you will need to transmit this key as well. We will get to that part a bit later.

The Flickr API covers a little over 250 methods. Some of these require you to be logged in with a Flickr account, but the others only require an API key.

For our purposes, we will be using a single API method called `flickr.photos.search`, which requires no login. This method looks for photos, based on some criteria. We will be using the current latitude and longitude of the device to get back photos within a specified distance from our current location.

Our search results come back to us as a big bundle of JSON that we will need to decode for display.

Once you have the API key, we can begin setting up our models, views, and controllers.

The SearchPhotos component

We will start building with our `search` component. To begin with, we need to add links in our main `index.html` to the files we will be creating. If you remember from the beginning of the chapter, we left ourselves some placeholders for adding in our models, views, and controllers. Let's add those in now, before we create the actual files:

```
<!-- Place your view files here -->
<div id="sencha-views">
<script type="text/javascript" src="app/views/Viewport.js"></script>
```

```
<script type="text/javascript" src="app/views/SearchPhotos.js"></
script>
<script type="text/javascript" src="app/views/PhotoDetails.js"></
script>
</div>

<!-- Place your model files here -->
<div id="sencha-models">
<script type="text/javascript" src="app/models/SearchPhoto.js"></
script>
</div>

<!-- Place your controller files here -->
<div id="sencha-controllers">
<script type="text/javascript" src="app/controllers/SearchPhotos.
js"></script>
</div>
```

The sencha-views section has our main viewport, our SearchPhotos (list) view, and our PhotoDetails view.

Our sencha-models section contains our SearchPhoto model that will be used by all our views.

The sencha-controllers section contains our single SearchPhoto controller that will handle communication between our views and models.

Now that these links are in place, we can start building the actual files.

The best place to start with new components is the model. Typically, if we understand the data we need to store and display, we can use that to determine how the rest of the application should be built.

The SearchPhotos model

Our search results will be constrained, in part, by the data we can get back from the Flickr API. However, we also want to display the images as part of our search results. This means we need to look at the Flickr API and see what is required to display an image from Flickr in our application.

If we take a look at http://www.flickr.com/services/api/misc.urls.html, we see that **Photo Source URLs** in Flickr has the following structure:

```
http://farm{farm-id}.static.flickr.com/{server-id}/{id}_{secret}.jpg
```

This means that, in order to display each photo, we need:

- farm-id: The group of servers the image is on
- server-id: The specific server the image is on
- id: The unique ID for the image
- secret: A code used by the Flickr API to route requests

These are all things that we get back as part of our flickr.photos.search request. We also get back the title for the photo, which we can use as part of our display.

Given these criteria, we need a SearchPhotos.js file in our models folder, with the following code:

```
Ext.regModel('FlickrFindr.model.SearchPhoto', {
fields: [
    {
name: 'id',
type: 'int'
  },
    {
name: 'owner',
type: 'string'
  },
    {
name: 'secret',
type: 'string'
  },
    {
name: 'server',
type: 'int'
  },
    {
name: 'farm',
type: 'int'
  },
    {
name: 'title',
type: 'string'
  }
  ]
});
```

We register our model, just as before, and then declare which fields we are using.

Remote loading

It's a good idea to get into the habit of using the full namespace of `FlickrFindr.model.SearchPhoto`. The next version of Sencha Touch will support remote loading for components. This means that you will not need to include all the files as part of your index. Sencha Touch will grab the component files and load them only when needed. It will do this based on the full name; the model is part of our main Flickr Finder application in the `models` folder and it's called `SearchPhoto.js`.

Next, we need to add some code to our `SearchPhoto.js` file, in the `model` folder. Beneath the `model` attribute, we need to add the following:

```
Ext.regStore('FlickrFindr.store.SearchPhotos', {
model: 'FlickrFindr.model.SearchPhoto',
autoLoad: false,
proxy: {
type: 'scripttag',
callbackParam: 'jsoncallback',
url: 'http://api.flickr.com/services/rest/',
extraParams: {
    'method': 'flickr.photos.search',
    'api_key': '783f66a1146d0be1ee5975785e6eb7a7',
    'format': 'json',
    'per_page': 25
  },
reader: {
type: 'json',
root: 'photos.photo'
  }
 }
});
```

Here, we register the `FlickrFindr.store.SearchPhotos` store, the same way we registered a model. We are using the `scripttag` proxy.

If you remember from *Chapter 6, Getting Data In*, this proxy type is used for handling requests to a separate server, much like JSONP. These cross-site requests require a callback function in order to process the data returned by the server. However, unlike JSONP, the `scripttag` proxy will handle the callback functionality for us almost automatically.

We say almost, because Flickr's API expects to receive the callback variable as:

```
jsoncallback =a_really_long_callback_function_name
```

By default, the store sends this variable as:

```
callback =a_really_long_callback_function_name
```

Fortunately, we can change this by setting this configuration option:

```
callbackParam: 'jsoncallback'
```

The next section sets the URL for contacting the Flickr API, which is `url: 'http://api.flickr.com/services/rest/'`. This URL is the same for any requests to the Flickr API. The `extraParams` setting is the piece that actually tells the API what to do. Let's take a closer look at that piece:

```
extraParams: {
      'method': 'flickr.photos.search',
      'api_key': 'your-api-key-goes-here',
      'format': 'json',
      'per_page': 25
   }
```

The `extraParams` are a set of keys and values that are posted to the URL. Notice that, unlike the configuration options, `extraParams` have both sides of the `:` in quotes. This can trip you up if you forget.

In this case, Flickr's API needs the following information:

- `method`: The method we are calling
- `api_key`: Our own personal API key (the one in the example is fake; you will need to supply your own API key in order for this to work)
- `format`: This is how we want to get the information back
- `per_page`: This sets how many images we want to get back from our request

Once we get our data back, we pass it to the reader:

```
reader: {
type: 'json',
root: 'photos.photo'
   }
```

Since we set `'format': 'json'`, we need to set `type: 'json'` in our `reader` function, We also need to tell the `reader` function where to start looking for photos in the `json` array that gets returned from Flickr. In this case, `root: 'photos.photo'` is the correct value.

Now that we have our data model and store set up, we need two views: the `SearchPhotos` view and the `PhotoDetails` view.

The SearchPhotos view

Create a `SearchPhotos.js` file in our `views` folder. This will be the first of our two views. Each view represents a single Sencha Touch display component. In this case, we will be using an `Ext.Panel` class for display and an XTemplate to lay out the panel.

Our XTemplate looks as follows:

```
FlickrFindr.view.SearchPhotoTpl = new Ext.XTemplate(
'<div class="searchresult">',
'<img src="{[this.getPhotoURL("s", values)]}" height="75"
width="75"/>',
' {title}</div>',
{
getPhotoURL: function(size, values) {
size = size || 's';
var url = 'http://farm' + values.farm + '.static.flickr.com/' + values.
server + '/' + values.id + '_' + values.secret + '_' + size + '.jpg';
return url;
  }
});
```

The first part of our XTemplate supplies the HTML we are going to populate with our date. We start by declaring a `div` tag with a class of `searchresult`. This gives us a class we can use later on to specify which photo result is being tapped.

Next, we have an image tag, which needs to include a Flickr image URL for the photo we want in the list. We could assemble this string as part of the HTML of our XTemplate, but we are going to take the opportunity to add some flexibility, by making this into a function on our XTemplate.

Flickr offers us a number of sizing options when using photos in this way. We can pass any of the following options along as part of our Flickr image URL:

- s: Small square, 75x75
- t: Thumbnail, 100 on longest side

- m: Small, 240 on longest side
- -: Medium, 500 on longest side
- z: Medium, 640 on longest side
- b: Large, 1024 on longest side
- o: Original image, either a JPG, GIF, or PNG depending on source format

We want to set our function up to take one of these options along with our template values and create the Flickr image URL. Our function first looks to see if we were passed a value for size, and if not, we set it to s, by default, using size = size || 's';.

Next, we assemble the URL using our XTemplate values and the size. Finally, we return the URL for use in our XTemplate HTML. This will let us create a thumbnail for each of our images.

Now, we need a place to put the template and our images:

```
FlickrFindr.view.SearchPhotos = Ext.extend(Ext.Panel, {
id: 'searchphotos',
layout: 'card',
fullscreen: true,

initComponent: function() {
Ext.apply(this, {
dockedItems: [],
items: [
        {
xtype: 'list',
store: 'FlickrFindr.store.SearchPhotos',
itemTpl: FlickrFindr.view.SearchPhotoTpl
        }
        ]
    });

FlickrFindr.view.SearchPhotos.superclass.initComponent.apply(this,
arguments);
    }
});

Ext.reg('searchphotos', FlickrFindr.view.SearchPhotos);
```

We create our `FlickrFindr.view.SearchPhotos` model by extending the `Ext.Panel` class. This panel will have a `card` layout, so we can switch between our list of photo thumbnails and a details page.

The `initComponent` configuration will set our `dockedItems` and `items` components for the panel. To start with, we only have a single `list` component, which uses our `store` and `itemTpl` objects, that we created previously.

The last two lines initialize the component and then register our new `xtype` attribute of the `searchphotos` component.

At this point, our application doesn't do much of anything, because the store isn't loading anything. We also have to tell the store our current location in order to get the photos nearby. It would also be nice if the application did this when it started up.

In order to accomplish these goals, we need to add a listener on our `list` component (after the `items` section):

```
listeners: {
render: function() {
var dt = new Date().add(Date.YEAR, -1);
var geo = new Ext.util.GeoLocation({
autoUpdate: false
        });
geo.updateLocation(function(geo) {
var easyparams = {
            "min_upload_date": dt.format("Y-m-d H:i:s"),
            "lat": geo.latitude,
            "lon": geo.longitude,
            "accuracy": 16,
            "radius": 10,
            "radius_units": "km"
        };
this.getStore().load({
params: easyparams
        });
    }, this);
}
}
```

Here, we have added a listener for the `render` function. This will fire once when the application starts.

In order to make sure we only get recent photos, we create a new `date` object that will hold the date one year ago, `(new Date().add(Date.YEAR, -1);`, for us to use later on.

We also set up a new `GeoLocation` object using the following:

```
var geo = new Ext.util.GeoLocation({
autoUpdate: false
        });
```

By setting `autoUpdate: false`, we only get the location data once. This will keep us from beating the user's battery to death by constantly updating our location.

As we have turned `autoUpdate` off, we need to manually trigger and update using `geo.updateLocation()` and pass it a function to run. The first thing our function does is to set up an array of Flickr API parameters we can then pass on to our store:

```
var easyparams = {
  "min_upload_date": dt.format("Y-m-d H:i:s"),
  "lat": geo.latitude,
  "lon": geo.longitude,
  "accuracy": 16,
  "radius": 10,
  "radius_units": "km"
};
```

The store takes anything we define as `params` and transmits it as a set of POST variables, as part of the load request. In this case, we send the parameters to Flickr's API and Flickr returns photos based on these variables.

The first parameter sets the minimum date for the photos we are interested in seeing. The other parameters set our current location via latitude and longitude from our `GeoLocation` object.

The `accuracy` parameter uses a range of 1 (World Level) to 16 (Street Level) and we have set this to 16. We are also setting a `radius` of 10 km for our search. We will play around with these elements later, in our advanced search.

Once all of our parameters are set, we still have one last thing to add, the `SearchPhotos` controller.

The SearchPhotos controller

The controller is where the bulk of our action code will go. Make a new file called `SearchPhotos.js` and put it in the `controllers` folder. Add the following code to the file:

```
Ext.regController('searchphotos', {
showResults: function() {
var results = Ext.getCmp('searchphotos');
```

```
results.setActiveItem(0);
  }
});
```

This code registers our controller and the first function sets the active item on our `searchphotos` container to our list (item 0).This function will be used as part of our **Back** button, later in the code. Let's give it a try in Safari.

If we load up our application in Safari, we will first get an alert asking if Safari can use our current location:

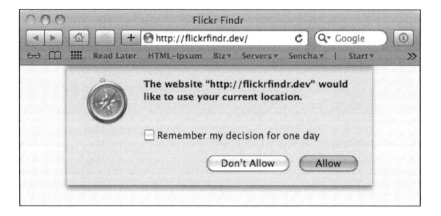

This alert allows users to decline the application access to their current location and ensures user privacy.

If you click **Allow**, our list will render and begin loading photos.

You should now see a list of photos near your location.

Flickr API explorer

If you are not getting back any results, you might want to try the Flickr API tester web page. This page will let you enter your parameters into a web form and see what you get back from the `flickr.photos.search` API request `http://www.flickr.com/services/api/explore/` `flickr.photos.search`. This will let you know if you are simply having a code issue, or if nobody has actually taken photos in your area.

Now that we have our photos working, it would be nice to see them in a larger format, so let's add our details view.

Adding the PhotoDetails view

First, we need to add the tap handler to our current list in the `views/SearchPhotos.js` file. This handler will swap our `card` layout to the details view, when an item in the list is tapped.

Underneath our listener for the `render` event, let's add one for tap handling:

```
itemtap: function(list, item) {
var photo = list.getStore().getAt(item);

Ext.dispatch({
controller: 'searchphotos',
action: 'showDetails',
args: [photo]
  });
}
```

As part of our function, we are passed the item number of the photo that was tapped. We need the actual data record from the store in order to display the details. We do this with `var photo = list.getStore().getAt(item)`.

Next, we use a method called `Ext.Dispatch()`. This method allows us to send commands and arguments back to the controller. In this case, we are calling `showDetails` and passing the photo record from the store.

The last thing we need to do in this file is add our details component into our items list. After the `list` component, add the following:

```
{
xtype: 'photodetails'
}
```

This adds a new component with an `xtype` attribute of `photodetails`. We will create this view after we add the `showDetails` code to our controller. We should be done with the `views/SearchPhotos.js` file for now. Let's move back to our controller file.

In the `controller/SearchPhotos.js` file, we need to add the code to display our photo in the `PhotoDetails` view (don't worry, we'll create that next). We can add the following new function after the `showResults` function:

```
showDetails: function(interaction) {
var photo = interaction.args[0];
var results = Ext.getCmp('searchphotos');
results.down('photodetails').update(photo.data);
results.setActiveItem(1);
}
```

For this function, we have been passed the photo record as part of an array of arguments, so we grab it with `var photo = interaction.args[0]`. Next, we get our `searchphotos` component and use the `down` method to find our `photodetails` item (which was part of the list of items in the `searchphotos` component). We then load the `photoDetails` with our photo data. Now, we can switch the `card` layout to show our details, using `results.setActiveItem(1)`.

Now that our controller understands what to do with the photo it's receiving from our `tap` event, we need to create the `PhotoDetails` view that will actually display the photo. This file should be placed in the `views` folder.

Our `PhotoDetails` view looks as follows:

```
FlickrFindr.view.PhotoDetails = Ext.extend(Ext.Panel, {
id: 'photodetails',
fullscreen: true,
tpl: '<h1>{title}</h1><img src="http://src.sencha.io/x100/x100/http://
farm{farm}.static.flickr.com/{server}/{id}_{secret}_b.jpg"></img>',
dockedItems: [
    {
xtype: 'toolbar',
items: [
        {
```

```
text: 'Back',
ui: 'back',
handler: function() {
Ext.dispatch({
controller: 'searchphotos',
action: 'showResults'
        });
    }
  }
  ]
}
],
initComponent: function() {
FlickrFindr.view.PhotoDetails.superclass.initComponent.apply(this,
arguments);
  }
});
```

```
Ext.reg('photodetails', FlickrFindr.view.PhotoDetails);
```

We start this file out much like our SearchPhotos view. We extend panel and give it an id and a tpl component.

We create the image link as part of the template, instead of adding it in as a function, as we did in the previous SearchPhotostpl model. This is simply to show that either way will work just fine. In this tpl component, we also added a reference to Sencha.io to resize our image based on the device:

```
http://src.sencha.io/x100/x100/http://farm{farm}.static.flickr.com/
{server}/{id}_{secret}_b.jpg
```

By using x100/x100, we can automatically resize the image to the full screen size of whatever device we run it on.

Next, we set up our dockedItems component with a **Back** button, so we can return to the list of photos. This button uses Ext.Dispatch to call the showResults function we added previously for the controller (the one that sets our card layout back to the list view).

Finally, we initialize our component and register our new xtype attribute, the same way we did with the SearchPhotos view.

Once we have the code for our view in place, we should be able to see our details by clicking on a file in the list.

Now that we can view our photos at full size, let's set up a savedphoto component that will allow us to save a link to any photos we like.

The savedphoto component

Our savedphoto component will need to store the information for a single photo from our search results. We will also need a list view for our saved photos and a details view, just like our previous SearchPhotos and PhotoDetails models.

Since our savedphoto model is simply displaying a subset of all of our photos, we can reuse a considerable amount of our code for this part of the application.

The SavedPhoto model

Since our SavedPhotos and our SearchPhotos models are storing the exact same type of data, we don't need to create a new model. However, we do need a separate data store, one that will store our SavedPhotos model locally.

Let's add a `SavedPhotos.js` file to our `models` folder:

```
Ext.regStore('FlickrFindr.store.SavedPhotos', {
model: 'FlickrFindr.model.SearchPhoto',
autoLoad: true,
proxy: {
type: 'localstorage',
id: 'flickr-bookmarks'
    }
});
```

Here, we just register our `FlickrFindr.store.SavedPhotos` class and reuse our model from `FlickrFindr.model.SearchPhoto`. We also want this store to load up when the application launches. Since it is grabbing local data, this should not present a huge load for the application.

We set our proxy to store the data locally and assign the store an `id` component, `flickr-bookmarks`, so we can grab it later.

Once you are finished with the `models/SavedPhotos.js` file, make sure to link to it in the index file.

The SavedPhoto views

For the `SavedPhoto` views, we need a list and a detail view. These views will be very close to what we already have for our `SearchPhotos` and `PhotoDetails` models. In fact, we can start by making copies of those two files and tweaking our layouts a bit.

In the `views` folder, make a copy of `SearchPhotos.js` and rename it to `SavedPhotos.js`. You will also need to replace all the occurrences of `SearchPhotos` and `searchphotos`, with `SavedPhotos` and `savedphotos`, respectively (remember that JavaScript is case-sensitive). Your code should look as follows:

```
FlickrFindr.view.SavedPhotos = Ext.extend(Ext.Panel, {
id: 'savedphotos',
layout: 'card',
fullscreen: true,

initComponent: function() {
Ext.apply(this, {
dockedItems: [{
xtype: 'toolbar',
dock: 'top',
title: 'Saved Photos',
items: []
```

```
          }],
    items: [
            {
    xtype: 'list',
    store: 'FlickrFindr.store.SavedPhotos',
    itemTpl: FlickrFindr.view.SearchPhotoTpl,
    listeners: {
    itemtap: function(list, item) {

    var photo = list.getStore().getAt(item);

    Ext.dispatch({
    controller: 'savedphotos',
    action: 'showDetails',
    args: [photo]
                });
            }
        }
      },
        {
    xtype: 'savedphotodetails'
      }
      ]
    });

    FlickrFindr.view.SavedPhotos.superclass.initComponent.apply(this,
    arguments);
      }
});

    Ext.reg('savedphotos', FlickrFindr.view.SavedPhotos);
```

You will notice that we did not include a template in this file; we are just reusing our FlickrFindr.view.SearchPhotoTpl class from the SearchPhotos.js file. It is perfectly fine to create a separate template, but reusing saves us a bit of memory and time.

Other than that, the file is largely the same as our SearchPhotos.js file: We create a panel with a card layout and add a toolbar. We have two items in the card layout: a list and a details panel (which we will create next). We set up our itemTap event to contact the controller and fire the showDetails function. Finally, we initialize the component and register an xtype attribute of savedphotos, for the component.

While it might seem a bit redundant to have two files that are so similar, it should be noted that they both read from different data stores, and they need to be addressed differently by the controllers. We are also going to make a few tweaks to the look of our different views, before it's all over.

For our `SavedPhotoDetails` model, we will take a similar approach. Copy the `PhotoDetails.js` file to your `views` folder and rename it to `SavedPhotoDetails.js`. This file will display a single saved photo. However, unlike the details for our search photos, this saved photo details panel does not need a **Save** button.

You will need to modify the file to remove the **Save** button:

```
FlickrFindr.view.SavedPhotoDetails = Ext.extend(Ext.Panel, {
id: 'savedphotodetails',
fullscreen: true,
tpl: '<h1>{title}</h1><img src="http://src.sencha.io/x100/http://
farm{farm}.static.flickr.com/{server}/{id}_{secret}_b.jpg"></img>',
dockedItems: [
    {
xtype: 'toolbar',
items: [
        {
text: 'Back',
ui: 'back',
handler: function() {
Ext.dispatch({
controller: 'savedphotos',
action: 'showSavedPhotos'
        });
    }
    }
    ]
  }
  ],
initComponent: function() {
FlickrFindr.view.SavedPhotoDetails.superclass.initComponent.
apply(this, arguments);
  }
});

Ext.reg('savedphotodetails', FlickrFindr.view.SavedPhotoDetails);
```

As before, this is much the same as the `PhotoDetails` file we created earlier; we have switched the names and changed our **Back** button to show our `SavedPhotos` list instead of the main photos list.

When you are finished with the two views, add them into the `sencha-views` class of our `index.html`, thus:

```html
<div id="sencha-views">
<script type="text/javascript" src="app/views/Viewport.js"></script>
<script type="text/javascript" src="app/views/SearchPhotos.js"></script>
<script type="text/javascript" src="app/views/PhotoDetails.js"></script>
<script type="text/javascript" src="app/views/SavedPhotos.js"></script>
<script type="text/javascript" src="app/views/SavedPhotoDetails.js"></script>
</div>
```

Now, we can move on to the controller for our `savedphotos` component.

The SavedPhotos controller

Create a new file called `SavedPhotos.js` in our `controller` folder. This file will have a structure similar to that of our other controller file; first we register the controller, and then we add functions:

```javascript
Ext.regController('savedphotos', {

showDetails: function(interaction) {
var photo = interaction.args[0];
var savedPhotos = Ext.getCmp('savedPhotos');
savedphotos.down('savedphotodetails').update(photo.data);
savedphotos.setActiveItem(1, 'slide');
    },
showSavedPhotos: function() {
var savedPhotos = Ext.getCmp('savedPhotos');
savedPhotos.setActiveItem(0, {
type: 'slide',
direction: 'right'
    });
    }

});
```

The first function, showDetails, is passed an array, called interaction, from our tap event (even though the user only taps one item, it is still passed as part of an array). We then grab our savedphotodetails component, by using the down method to search by id, and update the content area, using the data from the photo. Finally, we set the active item to 1, which is our savedphotodetails component, and animate the change using the slide animation.

If you remember, our showSavedPhotos function is tied to the **Back** button on our savedphotodetails component. This function selects the card layout for our main savedphotos panel (using Ext.getCmp('savedphotos')) and sets the active item back to 0, returning it to the savedphotos list.

Now, we need to add one more function to our controller. This one will allow us to pop up an alert when the user saves a photo and will ask them to name the photo. Since we only need a single text field, we probably don't need to create a separate form view; we can just use the Ext.Msg component.

Above the showDetails function, we need to add the following code:

```
addSavedPhoto: function() {
var panel = Ext.getCmp('photodetails');

Ext.Msg.prompt('Save Photo', 'Please enter a description:',
function(btn, value) {
if (btn == 'ok') {
var savedPhotoStore = Ext.StoreMgr.get('FlickrFindr.store.
SavedPhotos');

var savedPhoto = Ext.ModelMgr.create(panel.data, 'FlickrFindr.model.
SearchPhoto');
savedPhoto.set('title', value);
savedPhotoStore.loadRecords([savedphoto], true);
savedPhotoStore.sync();

var tabPanel = Ext.getCmp('viewport');
tabPanel.setActiveItem(1); //switch to the savedphoto view.
    }
  }, this, true, //multiline
panel.data.title, // value
  {
focus: true,
autocorrect: true,
maxlength: 255
  });
}
```

Our `addSavedPhoto` function first grabs the current photo details panel. This gives us access to all of the data currently stored in the panel.

Then the function shows off some of the power of the simple `Ext.Msg` component. Let's list out what we have here, before moving in for a closer look. First, by declaring `Ext.Msg.prompt`, we tell the message box that we are prompting the user to give us some information in a text field. Then, the `Ext.Msg` component sets the following:

- A title for the pop up
- The text for the pop up
- The function that received the button that got pressed, and the value of our text field
- A scope for the function (`this`)
- The value `true` (right after scope is set to `this`), which makes the text field capable of multiple lines
- A value to set as the default for our text field
- `focus`, `autocorrect`, and `maxlength`, which are three of the configuration options for the prompt configuration

The title and text are pretty straightforward, but let's take a closer look at the function. The function is called when the user clicks any of the buttons on the message dialog. The function is passed the name of the button that was pressed, and in the case of a prompt, the value of the text field.

To process this information and get it into our data store, we first grab the store using:

```
var savedPhotoStore = Ext.StoreMgr.get('FlickrFindr.store.
SavedPhotos');
```

Next, we create a new `savedphoto` component (`FlickrFindr.model.SearchPhoto`), using the model manager, and fill the data in with our current panel data (this is our current photo data). We also set the title to match the value the user entered into the message field:

```
var savedPhoto = Ext.ModelMgr.create(panel.data, 'FlickrFindr.model.
SearchPhoto');
savedphoto.set('title', value);
```

Once this is complete, we load the new `savedphoto` component in and sync the store to save our data:

```
savedPhotoStore.loadRecords([savedphoto], true);
savedPhotoStore.sync();
```

Once we are finished, we grab our main viewport and switch back to our `savedphotos` list:

```
var tabPanel = Ext.getCmp('viewport');
tabPanel.setActiveItem(1);
```

The rest of our `Ext.Msg.prompt` code sets the configuration options for the message box, providing the function `scope`, setting our text field to be multiline, giving a default value for our text area, and adding some additional configuration options.

This last group of values is called `promptConfig` and it's an optional set of configurations for the text area of the message box. Ours sets the focus on the text area (when the box appears), turns on auto-correct, and sets a maximum text length of 255 characters.

Multiline bug

There is currently a bug in Sencha Touch 1.1 if multiline is set to `true`. The bug causes the maximum length of the field to default to `0`, if you are using the Safari or Chrome browsers. The workaround is to set the `maxlength` to an actual number in the prompt configuration.

When you are finished with the controller code, remember to link to it in the `index.html` file:

```
<div id="sencha-controllers">
<script type="text/javascript" src="app/controllers/SearchPhotos.
js"></script>
<script type="text/javascript" src="app/controllers/SavedPhotos.js"></
script>
</div>
```

Now that we are done with the `savedphotos` controller, we can add the `savedphotos` component into our viewport.

Adding SavedPhotos to the viewport

When our viewport started out, we only had one item, the `SearchPhotos` component. Now that we have two separate lists, a tab panel would make more sense. Let's change the viewport.js code to look like this:

```
FlickrFindr.Viewport = Ext.extend(Ext.TabPanel, {
id: 'viewport',
fullscreen: true,
cardSwitchAnimation: 'slide',
```

```
        tabBar: {
        dock: 'bottom',
        layout: {
        pack: 'center'
            }
          },
        initComponent: function() {
        Ext.apply(this, {
        items: [{
        xtype: 'searchphotos',
        title: 'Search',
        iconCls: 'search'
                },
            {
        xtype: 'savedPhotos',
        title: 'Saved Photos',
        iconCls: 'favorites'
                }]
            });

        FlickrFindr.Viewport.superclass.initComponent.apply(this, arguments);
          }
        });
```

The first change we made was to swap out `Ext.Panel` for `Ext.TabPanel`, in our `extend` function.

Since the `TabPanel` needs a `cardSwitchAnimation` component for switching the tabs, and a `tabBar` component for showing the tabs, we added those as well.

Next, we added our panels for `searchphotos` and `savedphotos`, along with titles and an `iconCls` attribute for each. This will show up as part of our tabs at the bottom of the application.

The last thing we need to do is add our **Save** button, so that the user can save a specific photo.

Adding the Save button

The **Save** button needs to appear when the user is looking at a specific photo. This means we need to add it to our `PhotoDetails.js` view.

In the `views` folder, open the `PhotoDetails.js` file. Currently, our `dockedItems` component only has a **Back** button. We want to add a **Save** button on the right-hand side of the toolbar:

```
dockedItems: [
   {
xtype: 'toolbar',
items: [
      {
text: 'Back',
ui: 'back',
handler: function() {
Ext.dispatch({
controller: 'searchphotos',
action: 'showResults'
      });
   }
 }, {
xtype: 'spacer'
   },
    {
text: 'Save',
ui: 'action',
handler: function() {
Ext.dispatch({
controller: 'savedPhotos',
action: 'addSavedPhoto'
      });
   }
 }
 ]
}
]
```

We have actually added two items to our toolbar; the first one is a `spacer` component. The `spacer` component is a specialty toolbar component that shifts every item after the spacer over to the right side of the toolbar.

The second item is our **Save** button. This button's handler uses the `dispatch` function to tell our controller to run the `addSavedPhoto` function.

Once this code is added and saved, our application should be ready to use.

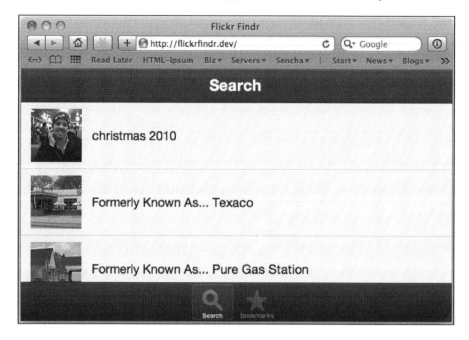

Polishing your application

Now that we've finished our application, we will want to add some finishing touches to really make our application shine and add a level of professionalism to the completed product. The good news is that all of these are easily and quickly implemented.

Animated transitions

One thing you'll notice is that, when we go from our SearchPhotos list view to the PhotoDetails view, we just jump from one to another via setActiveItem(). It can be a little jarring. In our SavedPhotos views, however, we snuck in some animations as the second argument to the setActiveItem() call. Going back and adding those same animations to our SearchPhotos controller will not only make the behavior more consistent, but it'll also make for a cleaner-feeling interface.

In the `controllers/SearchPhotos.js` file, find the `showDetails` function and change the following line:

```
results.setActiveItem(1);
```

Change it to:

```
results.setActiveItem(1, 'slide');
```

The `'slide'` animation will slide the `PhotoDetails` card in from the right, while sliding the `SearchPhotos` list out to the left. When we go back to the `SearchPhotos` list from the `PhotoDetails` view, we want to slide in the other direction. That takes a bit more configuration. Find the `showResults` function in the same controller file and change the following line:

```
results.setActiveItem(0);
```

Change it to:

```
results.setActiveItem(0, {
type: 'slide',
direction: 'right'
});
```

This will slide everything out to the right and in from the left, reversing the direction when we first went to our `PhotoDetails` view. There are more settings and animation types listed in the documentation, under `Ext.Anim`.

When you go from one web page to another, the new page simply replaces the old. But, in most mobile applications, moving from one view to another involves an animation. These sorts of animated transitions are easy to add and are important, because they help distinguish your application and make it feel more organic than a run-of-the-mill web page.

Application icons

As mentioned back in *Chapter 1, Let's Begin with Sencha Touch!*, users can navigate to your web application and then choose to save it to the desktop of their mobile device. When someone installs your application in this fashion, you can specify which icon is displayed on his or her home screen.

We've already got the code for this in our `index.html` file:

```
<link rel="apple-touch-icon" href="apple-touch-icon.png" />
```

Even though this says `"apple-touch-icon"`, most mobile devices, including Android devices, recognize the tag. Apple recommends that your application icon be 57 x 57 px, for some devices, and 114 x 114 px, for newer devices. It's safest to create your icon at a larger size, as it will be automatically scaled down, if necessary. Additionally, on Apple iOS devices, the corners will be automatically rounded and a glossy effect will be added.

If you want your icon left as it is, you can use the following tag:

```
<link rel="apple-touch-icon-precomposed" href="apple-touch-icon.png" />
```

The corners will still be automatically rounded, but the gloss effect will not be applied. Also, note that older Android versions (1.5 and 1.6) will only recognize the -precomposed tag.

 The text that's displayed on mobile devices' home screens, under your icon, will be whatever was placed in the <title></title> tags in your index.html file.

You can also specify different sizes of application icons for different device types:

```
<link rel="apple-touch-icon" href="apple-touch-icon.png" />

<link rel="apple-touch-icon" sizes="72x72" href="ipad-apple-touch-
icon.png" />

<link rel="apple-touch-icon" sizes="114x114" href="iphone4-apple-
touch-icon.png" />
```

This will allow you to customize the detail in the icon for different devices.

Apple iOS devices also allow you to specify a splash screen image that is displayed while your application is loading:

```
<link rel="apple-touch-startup-image" href="startup-image.png">
```

This image should be 320 x 460 px and in portrait orientation for iPhones. However, iPads can have different sized startup images, depending on whether they're in landscape or portrait orientation—748 x 1024 px for portrait and 1004 x 768 kpx for landscape.

You can specify different startup image sizes using media queries:

```
<link rel="apple-touch-startup-image" href="ipad-landscape-startup-
image.png" media="screen and (min-device-width: 481px) and (max-
device-width: 1024px) and (orientation:landscape)" />

<link rel="apple-touch-startup-image" href="ipad-portrait-startup-
image.png" media="screen and (min-device-width: 481px) and (max-
device-width: 1024px) and (orientation:portrait)" />

<link rel="apple-touch-startup-image" href="iphone-startup-image.png"
media="screen and (max-device-width: 320px)" />
```

Media queries are a powerful tool for specifying configurations based not on the actual device but on its physical characteristics, such as screen size or pixel depth.

 If you'd like to learn more about media queries, a good place to start is this article: `http://thinkvitamin.com/design/getting-started-and-gotchas-of-css-media-queries/`.

Try it yourself

There's still plenty of room for improvement in our application, but we will leave this as extra credit for the reader. Some things you might want to try:

- Adding paging, so that you can load more than the first page of 25 photos
- Adding an expert search, where you can set your location manually or widen the search radius
- Changing the theme and making the templates more appealing
- Adding the ability to save locations as well as photos

Try using the MVC organization techniques we have covered in this chapter, to expand the application and sharpen your skills.

Summary

In this chapter, we gave you an introduction to the Model View Controller (MVC) design pattern. We talked about setting up a more robust folder structure and created your main application files. We started our application with an overview of the Flickr API and explored how to register our various model, view, and controller components. We then set up our components for the `SearchPhotos` and the `SavedPhotos` models. We wrapped up the chapter with some hints for putting the finishing touches on your application and talked about a few extra pieces you might want to add to the application.

In the next chapter, we will cover a few advanced topics like building your own API's, creating offline applications using a manifest system, and compiling applications with a program such as PhoneGap.

9
Advanced Topics

In this chapter, we will explore a few high-level topics designed to point you in the right direction when building Sencha Touch applications, such as:

- Talking to your own server
- Going offline
- Compiling your application
- Getting into the marketplace

Talking to your own server

Up to this point, we have used local storage as a way to create a database directly on the device that is running our program. While this is very useful, it can also be limiting in a few ways:

- If any data is tied to the device, you cannot view the data from two different devices
- If the device is stolen/broken/lost or is otherwise unavailable, you also lose data
- Options for sharing are limited to transferring copies of the data
- Collaborative editing of the data is not possible

Each of these concerns can be addressed by storing the data in an external database, such as MySQL, PostgreSQL, or Oracle. These databases can run on the same server as our application, and they can handle multiple connections from different devices. Since all of the devices contact a single central database, sharing data across devices becomes much easier to accomplish.

Unfortunately, the Sencha Touch framework doesn't communicate directly with these types of external databases. In order to use a Sencha Touch application with an external database, we need to use a third party API, or create our own.

Using your own API

In the previous chapters, we have learned about using external APIs to work with data from services such as Flickr and Google. These APIs make it possible to grab data stored in the databases for these various services, but what about when you need to get data in and out of your own database server?

As it turns out, the best way to do this with Sencha Touch is to create your very own API. In order to do this, we need to step back and talk a little bit more about what an API is and what it does.

At its most basic, an API serves as a translator between the storage part of the application and the interface part of the application. The frontend makes a request to the API for data (say, a list of contacts), and the API pulls information from the database. The API then translates that data into JSON or XML and sends it back to the frontend for display.

While this might seem an unnecessary separation for an application, it actually has a number of benefits.

First, it allows the backend and the frontend to be written in different programming languages. This is important to us, because JavaScript, while it is a wonderful language for creating interfaces, is not a great way to talk with more robust database systems, such as MySQL, PostgreSQL, Microsoft SQL Server, or Oracle. The code for an API can be created in a database-friendly language, such as PHP, RUBY, or PERL.

We will be using PHP for our examples, but the choice of API language is entirely up to you. We are also going to be very general when covering the PHP side of things. Our goal is to communicate the concept rather than providing specific PHP code.

The second benefit is that multiple applications can use the API to access the data. This makes it much easier to share data between users and also makes it possible to provide completely different applications with the same data set (as the Flickr API does). We don't even have to care what programming language is used to build the frontend, as the API handles the translation.

Let's reexamine our `FlickrFindr` store to explore how this works:

```
Ext.regStore('FlickrFindr.store.SearchResults', {
  model: 'FlickrFindr.model.SearchResult',
  autoLoad: false,
  proxy: {
    type: 'scripttag',
    callbackParam: 'jsoncallback',
    url: 'http://api.flickr.com/services/rest/',
    extraParams: {
      'method': 'flickr.photos.search',
      'api_key': '783f66a1146d0be1ee5975785e6eb7a7',
      'format': 'json',
      'per_page': 25
    },
    reader: {
      type: 'json',
      root: 'photos.photo'
    }
  }
});
```

We pointed this store to a particular URL (`http://api.flickr.com/services/rest/`) and passed along a set of parameters as `extraParams`. We also passed along our location, radius, and accuracy settings, in the listener portion of our controller:

```
listeners: {
  render: function() {
    var dt = new Date().add(Date.YEAR, -1);
    var geo = new Ext.util.GeoLocation({
      autoUpdate: false
    });
    geo.updateLocation(function(geo) {
      var easyparams = {
        "min_upload_date": dt.format("Y-m-d H:i:s"),
        "lat": geo.latitude,
        "lon": geo.longitude,
        "accuracy": 16,
        "radius": 10,
        "radius_units": "km"
      };
      this.getStore().load({
        params: easyparams
      });
    }, this);
  }
}
```

Each of these parameters is sent along as a set of post variables to the Flickr API URL. Flickr then performs the function `flickr.photos.search`, using the variables we supplied. The API then assembles the results into JSON format and passes them back to us.

This is what is referred to as a REST request.

REST

REST stands for **Representational State Transfer**, which is an overly complicated way to say that we want to use the standard methods already built into HTTP in order to communicate. These methods allow HTTP to send data via `POST`, `PUT`, `DELETE`, and `GET`.

Sencha Touch version 1.1 is a strict REST implementation that uses these four separate methods to handle CRUD functions: `POST` handles the creating of new records, `GET` handles the reading of records, `PUT` handles the updating of existing records, and `DELETE` handles the deleting of records. (This will likely change with the next version, but for now, this is the way it works.)

If you have worked with forms on the web, you will likely be familiar with `GET` and `POST`. Both are used as a way to pass extra variables to a web page for processing. For example, `GET` uses a URL to pass its variables, such as the following:

```
http://www.my-application.com/users.php?userID=5&access=admin
```

This sends `userID=5` and `access=admin` to the web page for processing.

`POST`, `PUT`, and `DELETE` variables are sent as part of the HTTP request and do not appear in the URL. However, they transmit the same kind of data as key-value pairs.

Designing your API

It's a good idea, before you start coding, to think about how you would like your API to work. APIs can get complex rather quickly, and spending some time figuring out what it will and won't do can help you greatly as you build your application.

Different programmers have different philosophies on how to build APIs, so what we present here is just one possible approach.

Sencha Touch's models and proxies come with several methods, specifically the **CRUD** functions (**Create**, **Read**, **Update**, and **Delete**), which map quite well to API calls. This makes them a good place to start. First, make a list of what models you think you will need. For each model, you will need Create, Read, Update, and Delete.

Then, you should take a careful look at the models to see which may need additional API methods. A good example is a `user` model. You will definitely need the basic CRUD methods, but you will probably also need an authentication method to log the user in, and perhaps an additional method for checking permissions.

You may find, as you go, that you need to add additional API methods to specific models, but the standard CRUD functions should give you a good start at designing your API.

Creating the model and store

For this example, we will use a variation of the `Bookmarks` model and store from our `FlickrFindr` application, in the last chapter.

Since our `Bookmarks` component would now be pulled from a database, we need some extra options on the model. Instead of using the `SearchResults` model, as we did before, we will use a new model such as the following:

```
Ext.regModel('FlickrFindr.model.Bookmark', {
  fields: [
    {
    name: 'id',
    type: 'int'
  },
    {
    name: 'owner',
    type: 'string'
  },
    {
    name: 'secret',
    type: 'string'
  },
    {
    name: 'server',
    type: 'int'
  },
    {
    name: 'farm',
    type: 'int'
  },
    {
    name: 'title',
    type: 'string'
  }
```

```
    ],
    proxy: {
          type: 'rest',
          url : '/api/bookmarks.php'
      }
});
```

Here, we have added a `rest` proxy and `url` values to our model. This will allow us to save, edit, and delete, directly from the model.

For example, to save a new bookmark, we can call the following code in Sencha Touch:

```
var bookmark = Ext.ModelMgr.create({id: 6162315674, owner: 15638,
secret:'d94d1629f4', server:6161, farm:7, title:'Night Sky'},
'FlickrFindr.model.Bookmark');

bookmark.save();
```

This code will do a POST to /api/bookmarks.php, with all of our `bookmark` variables as key-value pairs.

Similarly, we can take an existing bookmark, change some of the information, and then call `bookmark.save()`. If we do this on an existing bookmark, the model will send the variables as part of a PUT request to /api/bookmarks.php.

As you might expect, calling `user.destroy()` will send our variables to /api/bookmarks.php, as part of a DELETE request.

We also have to modify our Bookmarks store in a similar fashion:

```
Ext.regStore('FlickrFindr.store.Bookmarks', {
  model: 'FlickrFindr.model.Bookmark',
  storeID: 'BookmarkStore',
  emptyText: 'No Bookmarks To List',
  autoload: true,
  proxy: {
    type: 'rest',
    url: '/api/bookmarks.php',
    reader: {
      type: 'json',
      root: 'children'
    }
  }
});
```

As before, the big difference with this store is the proxy configuration. We are using the same /api/bookmarks.php file to process our requests. In this case, the store will use the GET request method, when contacting the /api/bookmarks.php file.

Our reader has a root property of children. This means that the data coming back should look something like the following:

```
{
"total": 2,
  "children":[
    {
        "id":"6162315674",
        "owner":"Noel",
        "secret":"d94d1629f4",
        "server":"6161",
        "farm":7,
        "title":"Night Sky"
    },
    {
        "id":"6162337597",
        "owner":"Noel",
        "secret":"f496834m347",
        "server":"6161",
        "farm":7,
        "title":"Ring of Fire"
    }
  ]
}
```

Our store will begin looking for records inside the children array, and it will use the default variable of total to get the total number of records.

Making a request

Once our model and store understand how to make these requests, our PHP-based API file has to decide what to do with them. This means we have to set our bookmarks.php file to process the requests. At a very high level, this means doing something such as the following:

```
<?PHP
$action = $_SERVER['REQUEST_METHOD'];

if($action == 'GET') {
  // read - return a list of bookmarks as JSON
} else if($action == 'POST') {
```

```
    // add a new user
  } else if($action == 'PUT') {
    // save the edit of an existing user
  } else if($action == 'DELETE') {
    // delete an existing user
  }
  ?>
```

The `<?PHP` and `?>` tags simply denote the beginning and end of PHP code.

The `$action = $_SERVER['REQUEST_METHOD'];` line grabs the `request` method, and then we make our code decisions (`add`, `edit`, `read`, or `delete`), based on that result.

We don't want to get too far into code-specific examples, as these will vary greatly, depending on the language and database you want to use for your API. You will need to consult a guide for your specific API programming language, to learn how to interact appropriately with your chosen database.

One thing to note when performing `add`, `edit`, and `delete` functions is that the data that comes to your functions will arrive as an array of records such as this:

```
{"records":[{"id":6162315674,"owner":"46992422@N08","secret":"d94d1629
f4","server":6161,"farm":7,"title":"foo"}]}
```

This means that, for any `add`, `edit`, and `delete` options, you will need to loop through the values for each record and make your database changes for each one. While you could conceivably access the record directly with something like `records[0].id`, looping through the values allows you to take advantage of the data store's ability to sync multiple changes at once.

When your API sends back the results of the operation, Sencha Touch expects you to return the full record (or records) that were sent to the API in the first place. For example, if you create a new record, the API should, after a successful save, return that record as part of the results. If you modify several records and save them, the API should return all the modified records if they saved correctly. The reason for this is that it's possible that your API will make additional changes to the records that should be reflected in your JavaScript code. Returning the full records ensures that your JavaScript application stays up-to-date with any changes made by your API.

For example, we can add a number of bookmarks to the store instead of creating them directly through the model, as we did previously. When we call the `sync()` function on the store, it will send the data to our API as an array of bookmarks:

```
{"records":[{"id":6162315674
  "owner":"46992422@N08",
  "secret":"d94d1629f4",
  "server":6161,
  "farm":7,
  "title":"foo"},
  {"id":"6162337597",
  "owner":"Noel",
  "secret":"f496834m347",
  "server":"6161",
  "farm":7,
  "title":"Ring of Fire"}]}
```

This way, if we allow for looping in our API, we don't have to worry if the request came from the model or the store. From a receiving standpoint, the API only has to worry if the request is POST (add), PUT (edit), GET (read), or DELETE (delete).

However, there are also times where we need to communicate directly with the API and perhaps get back a more complete response. This is where an AJAX request can come in handy.

AJAX requests in an API

When working with an external database, there are often times when we need to make data changes outside of a specific model. We might also need to receive responses that are more complex than those available to the data store in the current version of Sencha Touch. In these cases, we can use an AJAX request object to send data directly to our backend for processing.

For example:

```
Ext.Ajax.request({
    url: '/api/bookmarks.php',
    method: 'GET',
    params: {
        id: '6162337597'
    },
    success: function(result, request) {
        var json = Ext.decode(result.responseText);
console.log(json.bookmark);
    },
```

```
failure: function(response, opts) {
        console.log('server-side failure with status code ' +
response.status);
    }
});
```

This code makes a direct GET request to /api/bookmarks.php and passes an id of 6162337597, as part of the request. The API can then use this information to grab a specific bookmark and return it to the AJAX request as JSON.

Success or failure is indicated by returning an appropriate HTTP status code. If you're returning a successful message, simply outputting JSON will return an acceptable status code. To indicate failure, you would return an error code in the 400 or 500 range. In PHP, that may look as follows:

```
<?PHP
header("Status: 400 Bad Request - Invalid Username");
?>
```

You'll need to look up how to send HTTP response headers in the documentation for your preferred API programming language.

 For a list of HTTP status codes, visit http://restpatterns.org/ HTTP_Status_Codes.

Going offline

Inevitably, people using your application will find themselves without Internet access. With traditional web applications, this typically means that the application was inaccessible and unusable. But with some careful planning, you can make your mobile application available offline.

Syncing local and remote data

The first thing to think about is your data: what data will your users need even if they are offline? Let's use a simple address book example. You would probably have a model for the contacts, and a store that queried your remote address book server, with perhaps a list view to display the contacts:

```
Ext.regModel('Contact', {
  fields: [
    {name: 'id', type: 'int'},
    {name: 'firstname', type: 'string'},
```

```
        {name: 'lastname', type: 'string'},
        {name: 'email', type: 'string'}
        ]
});

Ext.regStore('ContactStore', {
    model: 'Contact',
    proxy: {
        type: 'scripttag',
        url: 'http://mycontactserver.com/api',
    },
    autoLoad: true
});

var ContactView = Ext.extend(Ext.List, {
    store: 'ContactStore',
    itemTpl: '{firstname} {lastname} - {email}'
});

Ext.reg('contactview', ContactView);
```

> This is a very simple example, and we've left out creating an `index.html` file or adding the list to a viewport, even though those would both be necessary to make this application actually work.

You'll notice that our application uses a `scripttag` proxy, which is fine if we only wanted to load its data from a remote server. If we want our application to work offline, we will have to provide some local storage. Additionally, when the user comes back online, we will want them to be able to retrieve updated contact information from the remote server.

This means we'll need two stores, our current store, which uses a `scripttag` proxy, and a new store, to keep a copy of the data in local storage for when we go offline. The new store looks as follows:

```
Ext.regStore('OfflineContactStore', {
    model: 'Contact',
    proxy: {
        type: 'localstorage',
        id: 'contacts'
    },
    autoLoad: true
});
```

Our next task is to make sure that the offline store has the most recent data from the online store. We do this by adding a listener to the online store's `load` event. Each time the online store loads new data, we'll update the offline store. In this way, the offline store works as a cache for the online data:

```
Ext.regStore('ContactStore', {
    model: 'Contact',
    proxy: {
        type: 'scripttag',
        url: 'http://mycontactserver.com/api',
        reader: {
            type: 'json'
        }
    },
    autoLoad: true,
    listeners: {
        load: function() {
            var offlineContacts = Ext.StoreMgr.get('OfflineContactStore');

            offlineContacts.each(function(record) {
            offlineContacts.remove(record);
        });
        offlineContacts.sync();

            this.each(function(record) {
            offlineContacts.add(record.data);
        });

        offlineContacts.sync();

        }
    }
});
```

The `load` event is called whenever the online store successfully loads new data. In our handler, we first retrieve the offline store and clear it (otherwise, we would end up duplicating our data each time we loaded the online store). Then, we use the online store's `.each()` function to iterate through every record, adding that record's data to the offline store.

> **The .each() function**
>
> .each() is a function, provided by stores, that allows you to call a function for each record in that store. The function takes the individual record as a single argument. This allows you to perform operations on all the records, one at a time, rather than querying for them individually.

Now, every time the online store updates, the offline store updates, too. More importantly, though, when the online store is unable to update, the offline store will still have data in it. Since the offline store will always have data to display, even when the online store doesn't, we should use the offline store as the store for our list, so that we're always displaying something to our users. So, we change the ContactView variable as follows:

```
var ContactView = Ext.extend(Ext.List, {
  store: 'OfflineContactStore',
  tpl: '{firstname} {lastname} - {email}'
});
```

Our online store will still auto load when our application starts, even though it's not bound to our list any more, and if the user is online, all of the data in both stores will be updated.

Of course, there are other ways you could accomplish the same goal. You could use the Ext.List component's bindStore function to switch between the two stores, and the online store's scripttag proxy exception event to discover when you'd gone offline.

Or, you could look at the value of the window.navigator.onLine variable to determine your online state and set up your stores accordingly. We'll talk about both the scripttag proxy's exception event and the window.navigator.onLine variable, later in this chapter.

Manifests

Now that we've ensured that our data is available offline, we need to make sure that the rest of our application is available as well. This includes all of our JavaScript code, HTML, styles, and images. If our user has gone offline, they won't be able to load our application unless they've got a local copy to work from. That's where the Application Cache comes in.

HTML5 provides a mechanism for telling a web browser what parts of your application to store for offline use. This isn't a functionality provided by Sencha Touch, but it is something you should be familiar with, nonetheless.

The way you specify which files to cache is via a manifest. Let's create one for our simple address book application. Open up an empty text file and add the following:

```
CACHE MANIFEST
# Simple Address Book v1.0

CACHE:
index.html
app/app.js
css/my-app.css
lib/resources/css/sencha-touch.css
lib/sencha-touch.js

# Everything else requires us to be online.
NETWORK:
*
```

Then, save the file as `cache.manifest`. All lines starting with a hash (#) are comments and are ignored.

The first section following the term CACHE: is a list of files that the mobile device should save for offline use. If you have any images or other files that you use, those should be listed here as well.

The NETWORK: section lists all of the files that should only be available online. The asterisk (*) means everything not listed in the CACHE: section should be available online only.

 Most browsers limit offline storage to 5MB. This includes both the files listed in your manifest as well as any data in local storage stores. So, if you've got an exceptionally big application, you may want to be selective about what you allow your application to do offline.

In order to let browsers know about your manifest, you have to add a reference to it to the `index.html` file. However, this isn't done in the same way we link to CSS or JavaScript files. Instead, we add an attribute to the opening `html` tag:

```
<html manifest="cache.manifest">
```

Now, when you launch your browser, you should see our files listed in the **Application Cache**, in the developer console (Click the **Resource** tab and then the **Application Cache**):

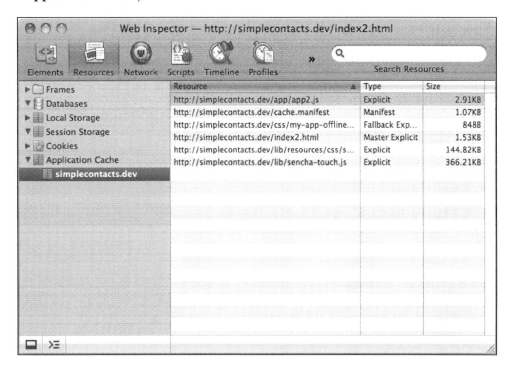

Setting up your web server

Initially, you may find that your manifest isn't working properly. Usually, this means that your web server isn't configured to serve manifest files in the way mobile browsers expect.

Web servers use something known as **MIME Types** to tell browsers how to handle certain files. MIME Types can get pretty complicated, but for manifests, all you have to do is add the following MIME Type to your server. You should consult the documentation for your web server for instructions, but we will take the Apache web server as an example.

For Apache, you should add the following to your `httpd.conf` file:

```
AddType text/cache-manifest .manifest
```

Then, restart your web server, for the changes to take effect.

For IIS, you will want to use the Administration UI to add the MIME Type.

 Take a look at the following links for setting up your web server:

- For more on setting up Apache: `http://httpd.apache.org/docs/current/mod/mod_mime.html`.
- For more on setting up IIS: `http://technet.microsoft.com/en-us/library/cc753281(WS.10).aspx`.

Updating your cached application

Once your application has been cached locally, the mobile device will no longer query your server to download your application files. This means that when you release updates or new versions of your application, users who've already cached your application won't get your updates.

The only way to force users to download the new version of your code is to update the manifest file itself. That's why we added these lines at the top:

```
CACHE MANIFEST
# Simple Address Book v1.0
```

Just update the version number and save the file:

```
CACHE MANIFEST
# Simple Address Book v1.1
```

This changes the manifest file, which will cause anyone with cached copies to redownload all of the files in the CACHE: section of the manifest.

 If you want to learn more about the Application Cache and manifest files, check out the *Beginner's Guide to Using the Application Cache*, at `http://www.html5rocks.com/en/tutorials/appcache/beginner/`.

Interface considerations

It's also important to let your users know when they're working in offline mode. Most devices have an online icon in a status bar, but even so, it's not always apparent to the user when they've gone offline. This means that you may want to let them know when you put your application in offline mode.

Alerting your users

In our address book example, we have an online store that updates a second offline store. The offline store holds the data that the user sees displayed in the Ext.List class. However, we never explicitly tell the user when they've gone offline. In our first example, we don't even keep track of online or offline status ourselves, because the application will work in either mode.

If we wanted to tell our users when the application has gone offline, the most reliable method is by waiting for the online store's request to time out. In the proxy, let's add a timeout component and a function to call when timeout occurs:

```
proxy: {
        type: 'scripttag',
      url: 'http://mycontactserver.com/api',

    timeout: 2000,
       listeners: {
         exception:function () {
    Ext.Msg.alert('Offline Mode', 'Network unreachable, we have
entered offline mode.');

       }
     }
}
```

The exception function will only be called after the timeout has elapsed. Timeouts in Sencha Touch are listed in milliseconds, so in this case, 2000 means two seconds. If the store doesn't get a response from the server in two seconds, the user is shown an alert informing them that the application has gone offline.

This is a good place to add other offline logic:

- If you've set up polling on your store, so that it automatically refreshes every so often, you may wish to turn it off
- If there are special offline UI elements, you can enable them here
- If you have a lot of offline logic, you will probably want to put the code in a separate function, so that you don't have to go hunting for it in the proxy configuration

If you are using the MVC structure discussed in the previous chapter, the controller would be a good place for this kind of logic.

Updating your UI

Another way to visually inform your users that they are in offline mode is to change the color or style of your application. While setting up an entirely different theme for offline mode may be overkill, there is a handy way to specify an offline stylesheet.

Let's create a file called `my-app-offline.css` and save it to our `css` folder. In the file, put the following:

```
.x-list .x-list-item {
  color: #f00;
}
```

This will turn the contact-list text red. Now, we need to load it when we're offline.

The Application Cache manifest file can have a section called `FALLBACK:`, which is used to substitute an alternate file when a particular file is unreachable. Let's add this to the bottom of our `cache.manifest` file:

```
FALLBACK:
css/my-app.css css/my-app-offline.css
```

You should also change the `css/my-app.css` line from the `CACHE:` section to reference `css/my-app-offline.css`, instead:

```
CACHE MANIFEST
# Simple Address Book v1.2

CACHE:
index.html
app/app.js
css/my-app-offline.css
lib/resources/css/sencha-touch.css
lib/sencha-touch.js

# Everything else requires us to be online.
NETWORK:
*

FALLBACK:
css/my-app.css css/my-app-offline.css
```

In the `index.html` file, you should leave `css/my-app.css` in the `style` tag, as that will be the file that's loaded when we're online. When we're offline, however, the manifest tells our mobile browser to silently use `css/my-app-offline.css`, instead.

Now, when your application is offline, it will automatically use `my-app-offline.css` instead of `my-app.css`. You could also use this to provide an offline version of images, or even of JavaScript files, if you wanted to completely segregate online and offline functionality. It should be noted that this method doesn't work if someone is online and then goes offline while using your application, say if they went through a tunnel and lost signal. In that case, you would want to use the event listener method to switch your user to offline mode.

Alternate methods of detecting offline mode

As mentioned previously, there are two alternate methods of detecting offline mode, the `navigator.onLine` and `online/offline` browser events.

The variable `navigator.onLine` will be true, if the browser is online, and false if it is not. In our previous `exception` function, we could add code to check it and change our message accordingly:

```
exception:function () {
  if (navigator.onLine) {
  Ext.Msg.alert('Network Error', 'We have an Internet connection, but
there is a problem communicating with the server.');
```

```
  } else {
    Ext.Msg.alert('Offline Mode', 'No Internet Connection, we have
entered offline mode.');
  }
}
```

Alternately, we can set up listeners for the browser's `online` and `offline` events:

```
window.addEventListener("offline", function(e) {
alert("Application is offline.");
});
window.addEventListener("online", function(e) {
alert("Application is online.");
});
```

You'll notice that we did not use Sencha Touch's event management here. This is because Sencha Touch does not provide custom events for `online` and `offline` events, so we have to use the browser's event listener function.

> Not all desktop browsers support the `navigator.onLine` or `online`/`offline` events, so, if you are making your application available to desktop users as well, you should use something like the timeout exception and manifest cache techniques, instead.

Getting into a marketplace

Sencha Touch applications offer developers a way to reach a wide audience using existing web technologies. Users can access an application via the web and even save it to their devices for offline use. While this flexibility is extremely valuable, you may also want to distribute your application through the various application stores available for Apple and Android.

In this section, we will take a look at some of the options available and the potential hurdles for releasing a compiled application.

Compiling your application

A compiled application is one that runs natively on the device in question. For Apple's iOS products, this means Objective C, and for Google's Android OS, this means Java. Both iOS and Android use their own **Software Development Kits (SDK)** to create these native applications.

An SDK is similar in functionality to something like Sencha Touch's framework, but they are much more complex and tied to a specific platform (iOS or Android). Since a native application is the only type that can be sold in the various App Stores for Android and iOS, we need a way to translate our Sencha Touch JavaScript into something the SDK can use.

Fortunately, Sencha Touch developers have a few options for translating their JavaScript-based applications into either of these languages and creating compiled applications.

The two most popular translation programs are PhoneGap and NimbleKit.

Both PhoneGap and NimbleKit use specialized templates that allow you to take your existing code and pull it into the SDK for iOS or Android. The templates create special folders and translation files that allow the SDK to create native applications with your Sencha Touch code. We will look at obtaining these SDKs in the *Registering for developer accounts* section.

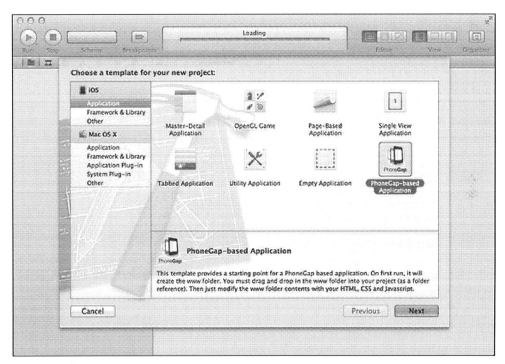

In addition to translating your Sencha Touch application to a native application, PhoneGap and NimbleKit also allow you to access some of the native features of the device. These features include things such as access to the file system on the device, access to the camera, and access to sound and vibration options on the device.

Let's take a look at these two options.

PhoneGap

PhoneGap offers a wide range of native functions through a global object called `navigator`. This object allows you to make JavaScript calls by using commands in your JavaScript, such as this:

```
navigator.camera.getPicture(...)
navigator.compass.getCurrentHeading(...)
```

The first command opens the camera on the device and lets your application take a picture. The picture is returned as a data string to your application, where you can manipulate it in JavaScript.

The second function returns the orientation of the device in degrees. This can be very useful in games where the play can be driven by the tilt of the device.

PhoneGap also offers access to:

- `Accelerometer`: Gets information from the device's motion sensor
- `Camera`: Takes a photo using the device's camera
- `Capture`: Captures audio or video
- `Compass`: Obtains the direction that the device is pointing
- `Connection`: Checks the network status and gets cellular network information
- `Contacts`: Works with the onboard contact database
- `Device`: Gathers device-specific information
- `Events`: Listens to native events on the device
- `File`: Reads and writes to the native file system
- `Geolocation`: Gathers more detailed location information
- `Media`: Plays back audio files
- `Notification`: Creates device notifications
- `Storage`: Stores data directly on the device

PhoneGap also offers options for compiling your applications for the Blackberry, WebOS, and Symbian platforms.

> Take a look at the following links for more resources on PhoneGap:
>
> - Download: `http://phonegap.com/download/`
> - Installation: `http://phonegap.com/start/`
> - Full API documentation: `http://docs.phonegap.com/en/1.2.0/index.html`
> - Step-by-step tutorial: `http://www.sencha.com/learn/a-sencha-touch-mvc-application-with-phonegap/`

NimbleKit

NimbleKit works in much the same way as PhoneGap, by providing a template add-on to the existing iOS development kit. The template allows you to move your code into a specialized folder that the SDK can then translate into a compiled, native application.

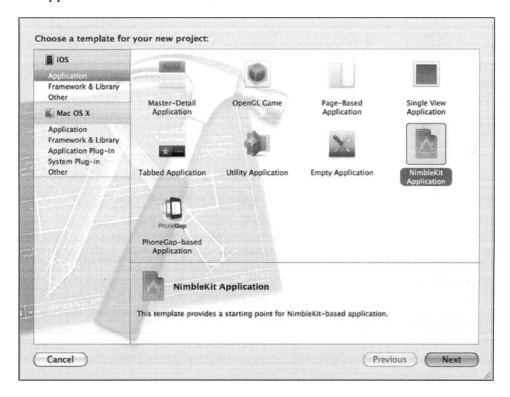

Like PhoneGap, NimbleKit also provides access to the native files, system, audio, video, contacts, databases, mail, and other device features. However, NimbleKit is specific to iOS applications and carries a price tag of $99.

Take a look at the following links for more resources on NimbleKit:

- Download: `http://nimblekit.com/`
- Documentation: `http://nimblekit.com/documentation.php`
- Step-by-step tutorial: `http://www.sencha.com/learn/enhancing-ios-sencha-touch-apps-with-nimblekit/`

Other options

Recently, PhoneGap launched a cloud-based service for compiling applications, called **PhoneGap: Build** (`https://build.phonegap.com/`). This unique service does away with the need to download the SDKs for each platform you wish to compile for. Files are simply uploaded to the Build service, and the system generates the application for the platforms you specify. This service is still very early in development but looks promising.

Additionally, Sencha Touch 2, with the ability to compile applications for both iOS and Android built right into the framework, has been launched. More information can be found at `http://docs.sencha.com/touch/2-0/#`.

As with any of these options, you will need to be a licensed developer on the platform you want to compile for. This can be a bit of a lengthy process, so let's take a look at what's involved.

Registering for developer accounts

In order to publish your application to the Apple Store, or to the Android Marketplace, you are going to have to sign up for their respective developer accounts. Both stores charge you a fee to become a developer and require quite a bit of information about you. They require this information for several reasons. First, they have to know who you are so that you can get paid for apps that you sell in their stores. Second, they need to know how to contact you if there's a problem with your application. And last, they need to be able to track you down if you try to do something evil with your application. Not that you would, of course!

In order to publish your application to either App Store, you will need to be a registered developer for that store. You will also need to download and install the appropriate SDK for that store, in order to be able to package up your application appropriately.

Becoming an Apple developer

To become an Apple developer, first you must go to `http://developer.apple.com/programs/register/`.

You will either need to supply your existing Apple ID or sign up for a new one, fill out some lengthy profile information, agree to some legal documents, and then perform an e-mail verification. From there, you will have access to the Apple developer center. The two points of most interest to us as mobile developers are the **iOSDev Center** and the **iOS Provisioning Portal**.

The iOSDev Center is where you can download the iOS SDK (known as **Xcode**) as well as read documentation, see sample code and how-tos, and view some videos on iOS development.

The iOS Provisioning Portal is where you add your application to the Apple Store or publish test versions of your application.

 In order to use Xcode or publish your application to the Apple Store, you must have a computer running OSX. Windows and Linux computers cannot run Xcode or publish to the Apple Store.

Becoming an Android Developer

Signing up for the Android Market is a very similar process. First, go to `https://market.android.com/publish/signup`.

There, you will be asked to fill out more profile information and pay your developer registration fee. You will also want to download the Android SDK at `http://developer.android.com/sdk/index.html`, although unlike Apple's SDK, the Android SDK will work on Windows, OSX, or Linux.

The Android Developer Dashboard also has links to guides, reference material, and instructional videos.

Summary

In this chapter, we covered a few advanced topics for the aspiring Sencha Touch developer. We first talked about creating your own API to communicate with a database server. We covered the REST method of communication for sending and receiving data from the server and discussed some options for building your own API.

 More resources on creating an API:

- How to create an API: `http://www.webresourcesdepot.com/how-to-create-an-api-10-tutorials/`
- Creating an API-centric web application: `http://net.tutsplus.com/tutorials/php/creating-an-api-centric-web-application/`

We then covered how to take your application offline using manifests and the Application Cache. We talked about best practices for alerting the user that the application is offline and about how you can detect the availability of an Internet connection using Sencha Touch and the device's web browser.

More resources on how to take your application offline:

- Taking Sencha Touch applications offline: `http://www.sencha.com/learn/taking-sencha-touch-apps-offline/`

- The HTML manifest attribute: `http://www.w3schools.com/html5/att_html_manifest.asp`

We closed the chapter with a look at getting into the application marketplace by compiling your application with PhoneGap or NimbleKit. We also talked about the process for becoming an Apple or Android developer so you can sell your application in the marketplace.

More resources on building Sencha Touch applications:

- Building a Sencha Touch application with PhoneGap: `http://www.sencha.com/learn/a-sencha-touch-mvc-application-with-phonegap/`

- Enhancing iOS Sencha Touch applications with NimbleKit: `http://www.sencha.com/learn/enhancing-ios-sencha-touch-apps-with-nimblekit/`

Index

Thank you for buying
Sencha Touch Mobile JavaScript Framework

About Packt Publishing

Packt, pronounced 'packed', published its first book "*Mastering phpMyAdmin for Effective MySQL Management*" in April 2004 and subsequently continued to specialize in publishing highly focused books on specific technologies and solutions.

Our books and publications share the experiences of your fellow IT professionals in adapting and customizing today's systems, applications, and frameworks. Our solution based books give you the knowledge and power to customize the software and technologies you're using to get the job done. Packt books are more specific and less general than the IT books you have seen in the past. Our unique business model allows us to bring you more focused information, giving you more of what you need to know, and less of what you don't.

Packt is a modern, yet unique publishing company, which focuses on producing quality, cutting-edge books for communities of developers, administrators, and newbies alike. For more information, please visit our website: www.packtpub.com.

About Packt Open Source

In 2010, Packt launched two new brands, Packt Open Source and Packt Enterprise, in order to continue its focus on specialization. This book is part of the Packt Open Source brand, home to books published on software built around Open Source licences, and offering information to anybody from advanced developers to budding web designers. The Open Source brand also runs Packt's Open Source Royalty Scheme, by which Packt gives a royalty to each Open Source project about whose software a book is sold.

Writing for Packt

We welcome all inquiries from people who are interested in authoring. Book proposals should be sent to author@packtpub.com. If your book idea is still at an early stage and you would like to discuss it first before writing a formal book proposal, contact us; one of our commissioning editors will get in touch with you.

We're not just looking for published authors; if you have strong technical skills but no writing experience, our experienced editors can help you develop a writing career, or simply get some additional reward for your expertise.

Sencha Touch Cookbook

ISBN: 978-1-84951-544-3   Paperback: 350 pages

Over 100 recipes for creating HTML5-based cross-platform apps for touch devices

1. Set up your production environment

2. Add life to your application using animations and media

3. Make your application available offline.

4. Engage users by responding to the events

PhoneGap Beginner's Guide

ISBN: 978-1-84951-536-8   Paperback: 328 pages

Build cross-platform mobile applications with the PhoneGap open source development framework

1. Learn how to use the PhoneGap mobile application framework

2. Develop cross-platform code for iOS, Android, BlackBerry, and more

3. Write robust and extensible JavaScript code

4. Master new HTML5 and CSS3 APIs

5. Full of practical tutorials to get you writing code right away

Please check **www.PacktPub.com** for information on our titles

jQuery 1.4 Reference Guide

ISBN: 978-1-84951-004-2   Paperback: 336 pages

A comprehensive exploration of the popular JavaScript library

1. Quickly look up features of the jQuery library

2. Step through each function, method, and selector expression in the jQuery library with an easy-to-follow approach

3. Understand the anatomy of a jQuery script

4. Write your own plug-ins using jQuery's powerful plug-in architecture

Appcelerator Titanium Smartphone App Development Cookbook

ISBN: 978-1-84951-396-8   Paperback: 308 pages

Over 80 recipes for creating native mobile applications specifically for iPhone and Android smartphones - no objective-C or Java required

1. Leverage your JavaScript skills to write mobile applications using Titanium Studio tools with the native advantage!

2. Extend the Titanium platform with your own native modules

3. A practical guide for packaging and submitting your apps to both the iTunes store and Android Marketplace

Please check **www.PacktPub.com** for information on our titles

16810718R00168

Made in the USA
Lexington, KY
12 August 2012